Analysis and Argument in First-Year Writing and Beyond

Analysis and Argument in First-Year Writing and Beyond
A Functional Perspective

SILVIA PESSOA, THOMAS D. MITCHELL, AND MARÍA PÍA GÓMEZ-LAICH

University of Michigan Press
Ann Arbor

Copyright © by the University of Michigan 2024
All rights reserved
Published in the United States of America by the
University of Michigan Press
Manufactured in the United States of America

Printed on acid-free paper

This publication was made possible by NPRP grant #8-1815-5-293 from the Qatar National Research Fund (a member of Qatar Foundation). The statements made herein are solely the responsibility of the authors.

ISBN 978-0-472-03977-7 (print)
ISBN 978-0-472-22193-6 (e-book)

No part of this publication may be reproduced, stored in a retrieval system, or transmitted in any form or by any means, electronic, mechanical, or otherwise, without the written permission of the publisher.

To our students and collaborators

Contents

Acknowledgments	xi
Preface	xiv

Chapter 1. Theoretical Principles for Scaffolding Argumentative Writing

1. Systemic Functional Linguistics and Genre — 1
2. The 3x3 Toolkit for Conceptualizing Argumentative Writing — 3
3. Understanding the 3x3 Through Analysis of History Arguments: The Importance of Interpersonal Meanings — 9
4. The 3x3 for Diagnosing Challenges With Argument: Challenges With Interpersonal Meanings — 11
5. Applying the 3x3 to Unpack the Process of Analysis: The Importance of Ideational Meanings — 13
6. Applying the 3x3 to Scaffold First-Year Writing — 17
7. How to Use the 3x3 to Scaffold Argumentative Writing — 20
8. The Teaching and Learning Cycle — 20

Chapter 2. The Onion Model: A Resource to Help Students Move From Knowledge Display to Knowledge Transformation

1. What Is the Expectation and What Is the Challenge for Students? — 24
2. What Does the Challenge Look Like in First-Year Writing and in Writing in the Disciplines? — 25
3. What Resource Can We Use to Address the Problem? — 26
4. Lessons — 28
   4.1. Moving From Knowledge Display to Knowledge Transformation Using Sample Texts — 28
   4.2. Identifying When an Assignment Calls for Description, Analysis, or Argument — 40

vii

viii CONTENTS

> 4.3. Other Activities for Identifying Whether Students
> Are Being Asked to Describe, Analyze, or Argue ... 41
> 4.4. Understanding Analysis and Argument Using
> a Visualization ... 41
> 5. Concluding Remarks ... 46

Chapter 3. Writing Effective Claims: Key Words, Evaluations, and Causal Relations

> 1. What Is the Expectation and What Is the Challenge
> for Students? ... 48
> 2. What Does the Challenge Look Like in First-Year Writing
> and in Writing in the Disciplines? ... 50
> 3. What Resources Can We Use to Address the Problem? ... 51
> 3.1. What Is a Claim? ... 51
> 3.2. Using Disciplinary Key Words to Write Claims ... 52
> 3.3. Using Language From the Prompt to Write Claims ... 54
> 3.4. Generating Disciplinary Key Words to Write Claims ... 56
> 3.5. From Isolated Claims to a Main Claim With
> Supporting Claims ... 59
> 4. Lessons ... 61
> 4.1. Which Claim Is More Effective? ... 61
> 4.2. Identifying the Components of Effective Claims ... 62
> 4.3. Analyzing Cases, Generating Key Words, and
> Writing Claims ... 63
> 4.4. Revising Claims ... 64
> 5. Concluding Remarks ... 65

Chapter 4. I Know, I See, I Conclude: Resources to Help Students Adopt Effective Patterns of Analytical Writing

> 1. What Is the Expectation and What Is the Challenge
> for Students? ... 67
> 2. What Does the Challenge Look Like in First-Year Writing
> and in Writing in the Disciplines? ... 68
> 3. How Can We Help Students With This Challenge? ... 71
> 3.1. The Know-See-Conclude Heuristic ... 71

Contents	ix

4. Lessons	73

4.1. Visualizing Information Flow to Avoid "Flatlines"
of Meaning · 73

4.2. Visualizing Effective Waves of Meaning · 76

4.3. Practice With Identifying Flatlines of Meaning · 80

4.4. Identify *Know, See,* and *Conclude* Moves · 81

5. Concluding Remarks · 85

Chapter 5. Engagement: Resources to Help Students Align the Reader Toward the Writer's Perspective

1. What Is the Expectation and What Is the Challenge
for Students? · 86

2. What Does the Challenge Look Like in First-Year Writing
and in Writing in the Disciplines? · 86

3. How Can We Help Students With This Challenge? · 91

3.1. The Engagement Framework · 91

3.2. The Big Effects of Small Choices on the
Reader-Writer Relationship · 95

4. Lessons · 96

4.1. Distinguishing Between Single- and
Multi-Voiced Texts · 96

4.2. Identifying Engagement Resources · 98

4.3. Revising Texts Using Engagement Resources to
Make Them More Effective · 102

5. Concluding Remarks · 103

Chapter 6. Justification: Resources for Justifying a Position Among Alternatives

1. What Is the Expectation and What Is the Challenge
for Students? · 104

2. What Does the Challenge Look Like in First-Year Writing
and in Writing in the Disciplines? · 104

3. What Resources Can We Use to Address the Challenge? · 109

4. Lessons · 111

4.1. Deconstructing Sample Texts to Show How to
Meet Genre Expectations · 111

4.2. Strategies That Can Be Used to Justify the Benefits of a Preferred Option or Alternative	118
4.3. Strategies That Can Be Used to Emphasize the Need to Persuade and Align the Reader Toward the Writer's Position	121
5. Concluding Remarks	123

Chapter 7. Tips for Assigning and Assessing Argumentative Writing

1. Overview	124
2. The Importance of Designing Assignment Guidelines and Prompts That Align With Pedagogical Expectations	125
3. The Importance of Word Choice in Prompts and Guidelines	125
4. The Importance of Avoiding Question Sets That Are Meant to Be Considered Holistically	130
5. The Importance of Having Consistent Parts in (First-Year Writing) Assignment Guidelines	133
6. Making Language Expectations Explicit in Assessment Rubrics	138
6.1. History Rubric	138
6.2. Information Systems Rubric	141
6.3. First-Year Writing Rubric	143
7. Applying the Teaching Learning Cycle: Drafting, Feedback, and Negotiated Construction	147
8. Concluding Remarks	148
Index	149

Acknowledgments

This book is the result of a great team effort. First, our deepest gratitude goes to the faculty across the disciplines from whom we learned a great deal. Their insights have been instrumental in our journey to articulate explicit writing expectations for students. The faculty welcomed us into their world, shared their writing assignments with us, opened their classrooms to us, answered our questions about disciplinary writing expectations, and challenged us to design writing materials that were accessible to the students. We are particularly thankful to Divakaran Liginlal, Cecile Le Roux, Ben Reilly, Aaron Jacobson, Alex Cheek, and Selma Limam Mansar. We hope that you keep the lessons learned with you and continue to adapt them to the needs of your classes.

We would also like to thank the students across the disciplines and the students in our first-year writing classes, from whom we also learned a lot. Their attentive participation in our writing workshops, thoughtful inquiries, willingness to share their writing for analysis, and responsiveness to our survey and interview inquiries have contributed immensely to our learning process. The students' writing confirmed the value of explicit instruction while helping us appreciate flexibility, diversity, and innovation in writing. Our analysis of student writing allowed us to revise our pedagogical materials to better help students meet assignment expectations.

We are thankful to Carnegie Mellon University in Qatar (CMUQ) and the Qatar National Research Fund (QNRF) for providing the support to carry out the research that helped us develop the writing tools shared in this book. Three major grants provided the financial support to do our research: CMUQ funded the initial stages of our research entitled "The CMUQ Study of Literacy: A Longitudinal Study of Academic Writing Development," and two major National Priorities Research Program (NPRP) grants from QNRF—NPRP 5-1320-6-040 Undergraduate Discipline-Specific Writing: Expectations, Demands, and Development and NPRP 8-1815-5-293 Scaffolding Literacy in Academic and Tertiary Environments in Qatar (SLATE-Q)—provided further financial support.

We also thank CMUQ for their financial support to attend conferences, share our work, and learn from experts in the field. The research office at CMUQ provided the administrative support to carry out our research project. We are particularly thankful to Maha Kanso and Maria Georges for their support with the institutional review board (IRB), budgets, and reports to QNRF. We also thank the Information Technology department for their continuous support, especially for supporting the design of a website in which we first showcased our materials.

Throughout our journey we were able to work with exceptional researchers who challenged us in ways that truly enhanced the quality of our work. Through our NPRP research projects, we worked with experts in the field and postdoctoral fellows who contributed to the success of our projects in many ways. We thank David Kaufer, who supported the initial stages of our research and provided a rhetoric and design lens to our work. Sally Humphrey and Ahmar Mahboob, coinvestigators and consultants in our SLATE-Q project, shared their knowledge, provided us with incredible support, and pushed us to use the Systemic Functional Linguistics (SFL) metalanguage all the way from Australia in weekly Skype meetings. Our postdoctoral fellows and collaborators Ryan Miller and Michael Maune worked very hard to make our ideas come to life. We will be forever grateful for everything we learned from them. In the early stages of our research, our undergraduate research assistants were very helpful with data management and preliminary analysis. Through publications of our work, several experts in the field and journal editors provided ample feedback to enhance our work. We thank Maria Estela Brisk, Nigel Caplan, Jim Donohue, Shoshana Dreyfus, Nigel Harwood, Alan Hirvela, Ann Johns, Emily Purser, Mary Schleppegrell, Christine Tardy, Sandra Zappa-Hollman, and Eszter Szenes.

At the University of Michigan Press, we are particularly thankful to our editor Katie LaPlant for believing in our book from the beginning and for providing support through the whole publication process. Katie and the reviewers' feedback helped us make the materials more accessible for teachers and students while keeping the rigorous language basis of our materials.

Last but not least, we would like to thank our families for their unconditional support. Our families in Uruguay, the United States, and Argentina offered support and cheering from a distance. Our partners in Qatar provided us with the day-to-day understanding, support, and

Acknowledgments xiii

listening ears that helped us through busy days in the classrooms with teachers and students, and long days analyzing student writing, working on presentations, writing for publication, and envisioning new projects. They also kept our homes and families running when we were away at conferences. Thank you Erik, Aymara, and Agustin! Silvia's daughters Leila and Olivia, and Tom and Pía's cats Vibra and Doha provided great refuge from the world of academia and taught us the genre of unconditional love.

Preface

This book is the result of over 10 years of research on analyzing, scaffolding, and assessing argumentative writing in first-year writing and disciplinary courses. The context where this work has been carried out is an English-medium branch campus of an American university in the Middle East that offers undergraduate degrees to students who use English as an additional language.

At university, learning is often assessed through writing, particularly through the writing of arguments in which students are expected to take a position by making an explicit evaluation or claim and provide reasons to justify their claims (Hirvela, 2017; Lee & Deakin, 2016; Wolfe, 2011). However, research shows that inexperienced and multilingual learners face difficulties writing arguments, and disciplinary faculty often lack the knowledge and expertise to make writing expectations explicit for students (Miller & Pessoa, 2017). When trying to write analytically or argumentatively, many students engage in *knowledge display* rather than *knowledge transformation* (cf. Scardamalia & Bereiter, 1987; Young & Leinhardt, 1998) and therefore may not meet genre or assignment expectations.

This book offers research-based tools for writing and disciplinary instructors to make argumentative writing expectations explicit for students. We have used these tools to meet the needs of students in our collaborations with faculty in various disciplines, including history, design, information systems, and organizational behavior. We have also adapted them and put them into practice in our own writing classrooms. As the number of multilingual students studying in English-medium universities continues to increase, the resources in this book can help teachers meet the writing and linguistic needs of their students.

To make explicit the linguistic resources of argument, we rely on genre-based pedagogy, which is informed by Systemic Functional Linguistics (SFL) (Humphrey, 2013; Martin, 1992; Martin & Rose, 2007,

Preface

xv

2008). SFL offers a way of deconstructing academic texts' schematic structure, that is, how a writer's social purpose is achieved through functional stages and linguistic resources. We rely on SFL because of its explicit focus on language and the tools it provides for studying and teaching school genres such as Argument. SFL-based instruction focuses on scaffolding students' production of different genres by making language choices explicit, and it has resulted in writing improvement, particularly for multilingual writers (e.g., Dreyfus et al., 2016; Humphrey & Macnaught, 2016; Mitchell et al., 2021; Pessoa et al., 2018).

The SFL tools highlighted in this book have helped bridge the gap between novice and experienced writers and have helped experienced writers develop in increasingly sophisticated ways (Mitchell et al., 2021; Pessoa et al., 2017, 2018). Through explicit instruction using these tools, students are able to progress toward writing effective arguments that draw on disciplinary knowledge to present and organize the information and acknowledge multiple voices and perspectives.

While SFL provides rich descriptions of language choices and other genre features, the metalanguage its practitioners employ can at times be daunting for the uninitiated. In this book, we aim to make our research-based SFL resources accessible for both teachers and students by showcasing tools that employ simplified, or "bridging," metalanguage. We explain these tools alongside mentor texts, sample texts, guided activities, and visualizations that cater to the diverse range of prior knowledge of the intended users. Teachers can adapt the suggested activities to fit their own contexts without seeing the resources as templates or prescriptive directives of what academic writing should look like. The materials offer a basis and a common language to talk about and teach analytical and argumentative writing that is useful for students, offering a foundation for novice writers and flexibility for sophisticated writers.

Chapter 1 introduces SFL and genre-based pedagogy, the theoretical basis for this book, with a focus on an SFL-based professional learning toolkit for making explicit the genre-specific linguistic resources needed for argument at the whole text, paragraph, and clause levels. The subsequent chapters focus on specific expectations for analytical and argumentative writing, articulating and illustrating the challenges students face when meeting those expectations, and providing research-based tools and activities for instructors to make genre expectations explicit. Chapter 2 focuses on resources to help students distinguish between descriptive, analytical, and argumentative writing and unpacks the process of analysis to help students write more effective analytical and argumentative texts. Chapter 3 focuses on resources to help students write effective argumentative claims. Chapter 4 focuses on resources to help students engage in analysis using a disciplinary framework. Chapter 5 focuses on resources to help students understand how to integrate outside voices to support their argument, use language to establish and maintain a consistent position, and anticipate and manage the reader's expectations. Chapter 6 focuses on resources to help students maintain a consistent stance while arguing for a preferred position among alternatives. Chapter 7 culminates with practical tips on assigning and assessing argumentative writing.

References

Dreyfus, S., Humphrey, S., Mahboob, A., & Martin, J. M. (2016). *Genre pedagogy in higher education. The SLATE project*. Palgrave Macmillan.

Hirvela, A. (2017). Argumentation and second language writing: Are we missing the boat? *Journal of Second Language Writing*, *36*, 69–74.

Humphrey, S. (2013). And the word became text: A 4x4 toolkit for scaffolding writing in secondary English. *English in Australia*, *48*, 46–55.

Humphrey, S., & Macnaught, L. (2016). Functional language instruction and the writing growth of English language learners in the middle years. *TESOL Quarterly*, *50*, 792–816.

Lee, J. J., & Deakin, L. (2016). Interactions in L1 and SL undergraduate student writing: Interactional metadiscourse in successful and less-successful argumentative essays. *Journal of Second Language Writing*, *33*, 21–34.

Martin, J. R. (1992). *English text: System and structure*. John Benjamins.

Martin, J. R., & Rose, D. (2007). *Working with discourse: Meaning beyond the clause*. Continuum.

Martin, J. R., & Rose, D. (2008). *Genre relations: Mapping culture*. Equinox.

Miller, R., & Pessoa, S. (2017). Integrating writing assignments at an American branch campus in Qatar: Challenges, adaptations, and recommendations. In L. R. Arnold, A. Nebel, & L. Ronesi (Eds.), *Emerging writing research from the Middle East-North Africa region* (pp. 175–200). University Press of Colorado.

Mitchell, T. D., Pessoa, S., Gómez-Laich, M. P., & Maune, M. (2021). Degrees of reasoning: Student uptake of a language-focused approach to scaffolding patterns of logical reasoning in the case analysis genre. *TESOL Quarterly, 55*, 1278–1310.

Pessoa, S., Mitchell, T. D., & Miller, R. T. (2017). Emergent arguments: A functional approach to analyzing student challenges with the argument genre. *Journal of Second Language Writing, 38*, 42–55.

Pessoa, S., Mitchell, T. D., & Miller, R. T. (2018). Scaffolding the argument genre in a multilingual university history classroom: Tracking the writing development of novice and experienced writers. *English for Specific Purposes, 50*, 81–96.

Scardamalia, M., & Bereiter, C. (1987). Knowledge telling and knowledge transforming in written composition. In S. Rosenberg (Ed.), *Cambridge monographs and texts in applied psycholinguistics. Advances in applied psycholinguistics (Vol. 1. Disorders of first-language development; Vol. 2. Reading, writing, and language learning)* (pp. 142–175). Cambridge University Press.

Wolfe, C. (2011). Argumentation across the curriculum. *Written Communication, 28*, 193–219.

Young, K. M., & Leinhardt, G. (1998). Writing from primary documents: A way of knowing in history. *Written Communication, 15*, 25–6.

CHAPTER 1

Theoretical Principles for Scaffolding Argumentative Writing

This chapter introduces the theoretical principles that inform both our conceptualization of argument and our tools and lessons for scaffolding argumentative writing in first-year writing and disciplinary courses. To conceptualize, scaffold, teach, and assess argumentative writing, we draw on Systemic Functional Linguistics (SFL), a theory of language developed by Michael Halliday (Halliday, 1985, 1994; Halliday & Matthiessen, 2004) that focuses on how language creates meaning, rather than how language is derived from rules. SFL describes how language is used within a social context, such as writing in a discipline. Our specific conceptualization of the Argument genre is informed by the SFL-based 3x3 professional learning toolkit (Humphrey et al., 2010; Humphrey, 2013), which aims to make explicit the genre-specific linguistic resources needed at the whole text, paragraph, and clause levels. Embedded in these theoretical premises, our approach to scaffolding argumentative writing relies on genre pedagogy and uses elements of the Teaching and Learning Cycle (TLC) (Rothery, 1996). Specifically, we use mentor texts to deconstruct genre expectations with students to help them with their independent construction of texts.

1. Systemic Functional Linguistics and Genre

According to SFL theory, language creates meaning within a social context to enact three language metafunctions: ideational, interpersonal, and textual. The ideational metafunction refers to the content function of language (Halliday, 2007). The interpersonal metafunction enables language users to interact with each other (speaker and listener or writer and reader). The textual metafunction involves resources to create an organized and cohesive message. When we use language, we choose from the linguistic resources from the different metafunctions, and our choices impact and are constrained by the social context. SFL posits that language is conceived as a whole text that exists in a social context rather than as isolated words or sentences. The recurrent forms of texts used by a particular community for specific purposes, with a specific discourse organization and language features, are known as genres (Martin, 1992).

SFL's explicit focus on language provides tools for the detailed analysis of school genres. Although variation between contexts is acknowledged, "within that variation, [there are] relatively stable underlying patterns of 'shapes' that organize texts so that they are culturally and socially functional" (Feez, 2022, p. 53), and thus genre instruction focuses on making language and language choices explicit and on scaffolding students' production of increasingly complex genres (Martin & Rose, 2008). Researchers who use SFL have applied these tools in the classroom, enabling teachers to make the language of academic writing explicit for students. Focusing on the contextual and linguistic elements that come together to create a text allows teachers to discuss them with students and help students identify them in the texts they read and write (Brisk, 2022). Educators who have used SFL to scaffold the writing of school genres have demonstrated its effectiveness in leading to writing improvement, particularly for multilingual writers (e.g., Brisk, 2022; Dreyfus et al., 2016, Humphrey, 2013; Martin & Rose, 2008; Rose & Martin, 2012). In our own work, we have also documented the effectiveness of SFL in helping students meet genre expectations in various disciplines (Mitchell & Pessoa, 2017; Pessoa et al., 2022;)

In university settings, Argument genres are prominent. In SFL, the Argument genre family comprises three types of genres: Exposition (argues for one position with supporting claims), Discussion (discusses multiple perspectives and argues for one), and Challenge (persuades the reader to reject another person's position).

In this book, we use the term *argument* to refer to Exposition because it is the most commonly assigned Argument genre at university and the one that is most familiar to instructors. In an argument, the writer puts forward a point of view in a thesis that is then developed with supporting arguments. Table 1.1 shows the social purpose, parts, and key linguistic features of the Argument genre. In the following section, we provide a robust SFL conceptualization of argument.

Table 1.1: Features of the Argument Genre

Social purpose	Parts	Key features
To put forward a point of view or argument	1. (Background) 2. Thesis 3. Supporting arguments 4. (Counter-arguments) 5. Reinforcement of thesis	Uses abstract nominal groups that name arguments and condense information; includes consistent evaluations; integrates and manages authoritative voices to support claims; aligns reader to the position advanced in the thesis; moves ideas from abstract to concrete in paragraphs with logical sequence

Note: Based on Coffin (2006) and Schleppegrell (2004). Genre stages in parentheses are optional.

2. The 3x3 Toolkit for Conceptualizing Argumentative Writing

In this section, we describe our journey developing resources aimed at helping writing and disciplinary teachers in their classes. Our work scaffolding argumentative writing using SFL had a pivotal moment when we came across the 3x3 toolkit, an SFL professional learning toolkit (Humphrey et al., 2010) that serves as the basis for the conceptualization of argument that informs this book. The 3x3 helped us investigate the challenges with argumentative writing in the discipline of history, and it paved the way for the rest of our work developing and putting into practice the tools highlighted in this book.

In our history writing research, we worked with an experienced history professor who expected students to write argumentative texts in response to prompts. The students were expected to respond to the history professor's prompt with an argumentative thesis and support their argument with evidence from the source texts. However, many students did not meet genre expectations. Many students were getting low grades and comments from the history professor that read "This is too descriptive or too narrative. This is not an argument." We found that many students were writing non-argument genres such as historical recounts, reports—genres that re-present information from readings as factual—or explanations—genres that focus on causes and effects without taking an argumentative position (Miller et al., 2014, 2016).

While the genre of most of these essays was easily identifiable, we were challenged by how to code a subset of them. These essays resembled arguments—they had an overarching argumentative thesis and were doing some argumentative work—but they had some features that were indicative of non-argument genres (Pessoa et al., 2017). In seeking to articulate what exactly was happening with these *emergent* arguments, we encountered the 3x3, an SFL professional learning toolkit (Humphrey et al., 2010) that would subsequently undergird our approach to genre analysis and genre pedagogy.

Figure 1.1 shows an adapted version of the 3x3 toolkit by Humphrey et al. (2010) and Dreyfus et al. (2016) for scaffolding, analyzing, and assessing academic genres.

The 3x3 toolkit can be used to describe the key linguistic features of particular academic genres by considering resources of the three SFL metafunctions of language: ideational (disciplinary knowledge), interpersonal (evaluations and authoritative stance), and textual (flow and organization), from the levels of the whole text, to its parts and paragraphs, to its sentences and clauses, as seen in Figure 1.1. Ideational meanings include resources for representing specialized and formal disciplinary knowledge, and resources for relating information in logical relationships (e.g., time, cause, consequence, comparison). Interpersonal meanings include resources for convincing the reader in critical yet authoritative ways. These include resources for incorporating source texts to further the writer's purpose and creating a consistent stance through evaluations.

Figure 1.1: General 3x3 for Academic Genres Adapted From Humphrey et al. (2010) and Dreyfus et al. (2016)

	Whole text	Paragraph	Sentences and clause
Ideational (disciplinary knowledge)	1. Do the beginning, middle, and end parts of the text build knowledge relevant to discipline-specific topics and purposes? 2. Does the language construct the technical, specialized, and formal knowledge of the discipline area?	1. Are topics defined and classified according to discipline-specific criteria? 2. Is information related in logical relationships (e.g., time, cause, consequence, comparison)? 3. Are tables, diagrams, lists, formulae, examples, and quotes logically integrated with verbal texts (e.g., to extend, report, specify, or qualify points)? 4. Is information expanded within paragraphs in terms of general to specific, point to elaboration, evidence to interpretation, or claim to evaluation?	1. Is vocabulary discipline-specific and formal? 2. Do noun groups effectively describe and classify specialized concepts (e.g., classifying adjectives, defining clauses)? 3. Do verb groups express processes relevant to the genre (e.g., defining, classifying, cause and effect, reporting)?

Figure 1.1: (Cont.)

	Whole text	Paragraph	Sentences and clause
Interpersonal (evaluations and authoritative stance)	1. Do the texts convince the reader by moving points or positions forward across the parts (e.g., by acknowledging experts in the field)? 2. Does the language present points and arguments in authoritative, impersonal, and objective ways?	1. Does the interaction with the reader focus on giving information (i.e., no questions or commands)? 2. Do patterns of evaluation develop the writer's stance within and across phases? 3. Are authoritative sources used to support points? 4. Does the writer include and control the voices of external sources to develop points and guide the reader toward a preferred position?	1. Is the text concerned with giving information through the use of declarative sentences? 2. Is the text objective in its presentation of opinions and recommendations (e.g., "It is clear that" or "There is a need for" rather than "I think or "You should"? 3. Do evaluations include degrees of intensity and attitude (e.g., very important, greatly benefited)? 4. Is source material incorporated into the text through correctly formed quotes, paragraphing, and summarizing? 5. Are sources cited correctly and referenced according to discipline specifications (e.g., APA)?
Textual (flow and organization)	1. Is the content previewed in the beginning part (introduction) and reviewed in the end state (i.e., conclusion)? 2. Are global headings and abstracts used to signal the layout of longer texts? 3. Does the language construct coherent, signposted, and abstract texts?	1. Are ideas developed within phases (e.g., paragraphs), with topic and summary sentences used to predict and summarize? 2. Does information flow logically from sentence to sentence across phases? 3. Are entities and parts of text tracked through cohesive resources (e.g., reference, substitution, and repetition)? 4. Does the text use connectors to create a logical flow of information and organize the text (e.g., repetition of key words, this/that, old before new, transitions)? 5. Does information flow from more dense abstract information in topic sentences to more concrete information in subsequent sentences?	1. Are abstract nouns used to present, generalize, and track ideas? (e.g., using nominalizations that convert verbs into nouns to express process: discovery instead of discover; reproduction instead of reproduce) 2. Is it clear when a new topic is presented? 3. Are articles and pronouns used to keep track of what is being written about? 4. Are sources cited correctly and referenced according to discipline specifications (e.g., APA)?

Textual meanings include resources for organizing clearly scaffolded texts, including resources for cohesion and a logical flow of information that moves from more dense abstract information in topic sentences to expanded concrete information in subsequent sentences.

The textual metafunction is the one that teachers tend to know the most about, and writing textbooks tend to focus on resources to help students organize their written ideas. In this book, we focus on tools for realizing ideational and interpersonal meanings, which involve language resources that are more challenging to unpack. It is these subtler features of writing, often realized at the paragraph level, that are vital to help students meet the expectations of analytical and argumentative writing.

Although the metafunctions are separated in the 3x3, "in practical terms, resources from different metafunctions and levels are typically combined to explore how meanings are instantiated in a particular text or set of texts" (Dreyfus et al., 2016, p. 111).

The 3x3 provides a conceptualization of academic writing that affords flexibility and facilitates adjustments to the expectations of the discipline and classroom where it is applied. The general 3x3 presented in Figure 1.1 can be adapted to a specific context, as we did in our work scaffolding argumentative writing in the disciplines of history, information systems, and organizational behavior, as well as in our first-year writing courses.

The 3x3 can help teachers—ourselves included—have a more robust understanding of the features of the genres they assign, allowing them to identify the subtle ways in which students meet or do not meet genre expectations. In our history research, we designed a specific 3x3 for history arguments (Figure 1.2), which allowed us to unpack what was happening in the emergent arguments and to identify the subtle ways in which students were not meeting genre expectations. In the following two sections, we unpack these features in effective (Text 1) and emergent (Text 2) history arguments.

Figure 1.2: 3x3 to Analyze History Arguments

	Whole text	Paragraph	Sentences and clause
Ideational	1. The text is grounded in accurate and relevant knowledge and language from the source text and the discipline.	1. The text uses a clear analytical framework (overarching claim with subclaims) to present information according to the demands of the prompt.	1. Specialized/technical vocabulary is used to characterize an overarching claim.

Theoretical Principles for Scaffolding Argumentative Writing 7

Figure 1.2: (Cont.)

	Whole text	Paragraph	Sentences and clause
	2. Ideas are developed through discipline-specific topics and subtopics to form an analytical framework. 3. The answer to the prompt is consistent from beginning to end.	2. Related topics are grouped as distinct supporting claims. 3. Information related to one topic is expanded as the text integrates accurate, relevant, and sufficient content from the source text. 4. Information is expanded within paragraphs in terms of general to specific, point to elaboration, evidence to interpretation, or claim to evaluation. 5. Information is related in logical relationships to further a claim (e.g., cause, consequence, comparison). 6. Examples and quotes are logically integrated in the text to support claims.	2. Abstract nouns are used in the introduction and in the topic sentences to create a taxonomy for the subclaims. 3. Vocabulary is discipline-specific and formal. 4. Causal and contrasting conjunctions and text connectives expand and link ideas logically (e.g., *because, so, thus, therefore, but, however*).
Interpersonal	1. The text answers the prompt with a defendable overarching proposition that shows interpretations of history as tentative (not factual) and as something that must be argued for. 2. The proposition is reinforced, justified, and defended to persuade the reader that a position is valid.	1. The text includes and controls external voices (e.g., the source text) to develop points, include evidence, and show how the evidence supports the claims. 2. The text acknowledges different perspectives and guides the reader toward the overarching claim.	1. The text justifies reasons (e.g., *This obstacle is important because . . .*). 2. The text integrates the source text (e.g., *The author argues . . . . According to the author . . .*). 3. The text shows how the information supports the thesis and supporting claims (e.g., *this shows, this means, this evidence is indicative of . . .*).

(Continued)

Figure 1.2: (Cont.)

	Whole text	Paragraph	Sentences and clause
	3. The text moves its points or positions forward across the stages using the source text as evidence for claims. 4. The text consistently guides the reader toward the overarching claim.	3. Consistent evaluations are used within and across paragraphs.	4. The text consistently supports the argument while showing awareness of and/or refuting alternative perspectives using modality (e.g., *may, can, seem, possibly*), concede-counter moves (e.g., *although this . . . that*), and counter moves (e.g., *even, just, only, although*).
Textual	1. The text previews the claims to be discussed in the introduction, includes supporting arguments in the body paragraphs, and reiterates the points in the conclusion. 2. The text creates coherence by predicting, signposting, and scaffolding ideas.	1. The language and order of subclaims in the body paragraphs match the preview in the introduction. 2. Subclaims are placed at the beginning of the paragraphs. 3. Paragraphs are developed in focus from general and abstract in "packed" topic sentences to specific and concrete in "unpacked" sentences. 4. The text uses connectors to create a logical flow of information (e.g., repetition of key words, this/that, old before new, transitions).	1. Abstract nouns are used to pack, signal, or foreground information and track ideas.

3. Understanding the 3x3 Through Analysis of History Arguments: The Importance of Interpersonal Meanings

In this section, we unpack the key resources of an effective history argument (Text 1) using our 3x3 and emphasize the importance of interpersonal resources for this genre.

TEXT 1: Effective Argumentative Essay From a History Course

Prompt: Based on your interpretation of Hammurabi's Code, how would you characterize the social structure of Babylonia?

Thesis: Hammurabi's Code indicates a distinct social hierarchy present in ancient Babylonia and suggests that certain social classes were viewed superior to others as perceived in the different punishments and rewards based on social class.

Paragraph 1: In Hammurabi's Code, laws that established punishments for certain crimes indicate that certain social classes are given preference over others. . . .

Paragraph 2: Laws that established rewards for certain actions indicate different levels of social class superiority in the ancient Babylonian social structure. This is evident in rewards offered to physicians for treating patients of different social classes. For example, Law 215 states that "if a physician saves the patient's eye, he shall receive ten shekels in money (215)." However, the subsequent laws add that "if the patient be a freed man, he (the physician) receives five shekels, and if the patient is a slave, the physician receives two shekels (216–217)." This is indicative of an attempt to assign a monetary value to an individual's health and suggests that a free man's health is worth five times more than a slave's health. Thus, one can assume that a free man is superior to a freed man, and a freed man is superior to a slave, indicating a social hierarchy. Although some may view this law as fair because payment was based on the wealth of the patient, it actually promoted unequal health treatment as physicians first attended to the needs of upperclassmen while neglecting the needs of lower-class people.

In terms of ideational meanings, Text 1 starts with an introduction that has an overarching claim and subclaims to present information in response to the prompt. The writer responds to the prompt's invitation to characterize and evaluate Babylonia's social structure (*a distinct social hierarchy*) and states the supporting claims (*different punishments and rewards based on social class*). In terms of textual meanings, the writer previews the supporting claims in the introduction (*different punishments and rewards based on social class*) and presents one supporting claim in one body paragraph and the other supporting claim in the next body paragraph. The text shows an awareness of the importance of following, predicting, signposting, and scaffolding ideas through the use of nominal expressions to pack, signal, foreground, and track ideas (evident in the consistent focus on social class differences throughout).

In terms of interpersonal meanings, Text 1 uses evidence and strategically manages multiple voices to develop points, include evidence, show how the evidence supports the claims, and persuade a potentially resistant reader. The writer does this by integrating the authoritative voice of the source (*For example, Law 215*) and by explaining the quote as it relates to the writer's argument (*this is indicative of*), thus bringing the reader closer to the writer's perspective. The strategic use of these resources restricts the possible interpretations of the evidence to that of the writer, thereby bringing the reader closer to the writer's perspective. Another way Text 1 strategically manages multiple voices is with a concede-counter move that can make resistant readers more receptive: *Although some may view this law as fair because . . . it promoted unequal health treatment . . . .* By conceding that it is understandable that someone might interpret things one way, the writer expands the dialog and gives up some ground to an alternative perspective. With the counter that follows, the writer brings the reader toward their position. In our research, we have found that interpersonal resources are of great importance in history arguments, but students face challenges incorporating these resources in their writing, as shown in the next section.

Figure 1.3 shows Text 1 annotated with the key features of Argument. These features are described here in general terms. More detailed SFL descriptions of the language of these features will be discussed in subsequent chapters in this book.

Figure 1.3: Effective Argumentative History Essay Annotated With the Key Features of Argument

Prompt: Based on your interpretation of Hammurabi's Code, how would you characterize the social structure of Babylonia?	
Hammurabi's Code indicates a distinct social hierarchy present in ancient Babylonia and suggests that certain social classes were viewed superior to others as perceived in the different punishments and rewards based on social class.	**Thesis Stage:** *States main argument and previews Arguments 1 and 2
In Hammurabi's Code, laws that established punishments for certain crimes indicate that certain social classes are given preference over others. . . .	**Supporting Claim 1**

Theoretical Principles for Scaffolding Argumentative Writing

Figure 1.3: (Cont.)

Laws that established rewards for certain actions indicate different levels of social class superiority in the ancient Babylonian social structure.	Supporting Claim 2
This is evident in rewards offered to physicians for treating patients of different social classes.	*Elaborating evidence
For example, Law 215 states that "if a physician saves the patient's eye, he shall receive ten shekels in money (215)." However, the subsequent laws add that "if the patient be a freed man, he (the physician) receives five shekels, and if the patient is a slave, the physician receives two shekels (216–217)."	*Controls external voice (from course reading) to develop points
This is indicative of an attempt to assign a monetary value to an individual's health and suggests that a free man's health is worth five times more than a slave's health. Thus, one can assume that a free man is superior to a freed man, and a freed man is superior to a slave, indicating a social hierarchy.	*Shows how the evidence supports the claim
Although some may view this law as fair because payment was based on the wealth of the patient, it actually promoted unequal health treatment as physicians first attended to the needs of upperclassmen while neglecting the needs of lower-class people.	*Concession to acknowledge potential opposing view followed by counter to align the reader

4. The 3x3 for Diagnosing Challenges With Argument: Challenges With Interpersonal Meanings

The 3x3 helped us identify effective argument in history, as in Text 1. Most importantly, the 3x3 helped us identify what linguistic features were missing in the history essays that looked like arguments but were not fully meeting genre expectations. We call these essays *emergent* arguments: essays that have a viable overarching claim and some support but do not adequately control the resources of all three metafunctions (Pessoa et al., 2017).

TEXT 2: Emergent Argument With Ineffective Use of Interpersonal Resources

Prompt: Based on your interpretation of Hammurabi's Code, how would you characterize the social structure of Babylonia?

Thesis: Hammurabi's Code indicates a distinct social hierarchy present in ancient Babylonia and suggests that certain social classes were viewed superior to others as perceived in the different punishments and rewards based on social class.

Paragraph 1: The first social class in Babylonia is the free upper-class people. . . .

Paragraph 2: Below the free upper-class people in Ancient Babylonia are the class of freed men. The freed men were former slaves who became free or men from the upper class who committed mistakes and were punished by losing their status. People from this class received different treatment from people from the upper-class people. A doctor would receive 5 shekels for treating a freed man . . .

In terms of ideational and textual meanings, like Text 1, Text 2 looks like an argument. The writer includes a thesis statement that effectively responds to the prompt's invitation to characterize and evaluate Babylonia's social structure (*a distinct social hierarchy*) and previews the supporting claims that logically follow from the thesis (*different punishments and rewards based on social class*). The text follows this organization by first presenting one supporting claim in one body paragraph and then the other in the next body paragraph.

However, Text 2 falls short of meeting genre expectations regarding interpersonal meanings. While the text has a thesis that takes a position that can be defended, the rest of the text falls back into knowledge display: the writer reports information from the source text without citing it directly or linking the information back to the thesis to show how it supports the overall position. There are no indications, apart from the thesis, that the writer anticipates a reader who might disagree with their interpretation of historical knowledge. In other words, after the thesis, Text 2 presents historical information as factual, a characteristic of non-argument historical genres where the focus is on providing "relatively categorical explanations of historical phenomena" (Coffin, 2006, p. 77). This type of writing is reminiscent of high school history textbooks, where the rhetorical goal is not to persuade the readers that events happened in the way described or anticipate objections to a particular version of events but to provide an uncontested account of history that the reader will take to be factual. When students are asked to write arguments based on a source text, the professor does not want to see the writer explain its content as if it were unquestionably true. Student responses like Text 2 reveal how challenging it can be for students to write arguments and indicate the importance of being explicit about the interpersonal resources needed to write arguments in history.

Without a 3x3 conceptualization of argument, a teacher reading Text 2 quickly may miss the important ways in which this essay does not meet genre expectations. If teachers only focus on the introduction, thesis statement, preview of the supporting claims, and the topic sentences, then Text 2 could easily "pass" as an effective argument. However, a closer look at the body paragraphs indicates that Text 2 does not effectively use interpersonal resources that are key to argument in history.

In our research, we have also encountered *emergent arguments* in history that were doing argumentative work through the use of interpersonal resources but did not fully control ideational or textual meanings. In terms of ideational resources, the student would, for example, preview supporting claims in the introduction but would write about other topics in the body paragraphs. Regarding textual resources, the student would, for example, fail to preview the supporting claims and would write paragraphs that started with evidence or examples without an effective topic sentence and proper paragraph development from general to specific. Without a 3x3 conceptualization of argument, a teacher might dismiss these essays as "disorganized" or "messy" and might not acknowledge all the interesting argumentative work that might happen inside the paragraphs.

A 3x3 conceptualization of argument can help teachers diagnose challenges with argument and understand where to focus instruction and students' attention. In history, we have found that while students have an easier time controlling ideational and textual meanings, the control of interpersonal meanings is more difficult, and more attention needs to be given to these resources. Chapters 5 and 6 provide tools for using interpersonal resources in argument. In genres in other disciplines, we have found that ideational meanings are of critical importance to meet genre expectations, as discussed in the next section.

5. Applying the 3x3 to Unpack the Process of Analysis: The Importance of Ideational Meanings

In order to write effective arguments, students must engage in the process of analysis. When students analyze, they reorganize information in some original way for the purposes of the text, often by applying a disciplinary framework to a case or an example (Humphrey & Economou, 2015). Disciplinary frameworks may be thought of as a discipline's agreed-upon classificatory and compositional schemes or, in other words, its analytical lenses. Analytical writing is organized by the elements of the disciplinary framework—that is, sentences and paragraphs are often grouped together based on the relevant components of the framework.

A disciplinary framework fits into the ideational meanings category of the general 3x3 from Figure 1.1. A disciplinary framework is the technical, specialized, and formal knowledge of a discipline that is used to classify, present, and organize the information in a text. Each discipline has its own sets of disciplinary frameworks. For example, in a writing class, instructors might use Toulmin's Argument Model as a disciplinary framework that students apply to analyze an argument to determine its *claims*, *grounds*, and *warrants*. In a document design class, a student might analyze a document's use of *contrast*, *repetition*, *alignment*, and *proximity*. In each of these examples, the student needs to parse the relevant details of the object of analysis and determine how they relate to the elements of the disciplinary framework.

One particular genre in which the application of a disciplinary framework is integral to meeting expectations and where controlling ideational meanings is vital is the Case Analysis. A Case Analysis is a genre that includes analysis of an organization, using disciplinary concepts to identify problems or opportunities in a case, followed by recommendations for enhancing the organization's practices. The Case Analysis is an argumentative text because it requires an overarching claim about the problems or opportunities identified in the organization; an analysis of the organization that uses evidence from the case to support the overall claim; and recommendations, which follow from the analysis and must be justified as the best way to solve the identified problems or act on the opportunities.

While interpersonal resources are important for writing an effective Case Analysis (like in all arguments), ideational resources are especially important for the analysis section, where key concepts from the disciplinary knowledge are used as the analytical framework to present, organize, and develop the information and the claims in the text (Pessoa et al., 2019).

For example, Text 3 shows an excerpt from a mentor text that we have used to scaffold the Case Analysis in an organizational behavior course. In the paragraph provided, we use the framework of leadership style to analyze the problems with the leadership at M University.

TEXT 3: Excerpt From a Mentor Case Analysis With Key Features of Argument

At M University (MU), the new leadership seems to have had a negative impact on the university. The new leadership's style, lack of diversity, and priorities have impacted the culture of accomplishment of the university and the motivation and retention of its once highly accomplished and diverse faculty, with potential consequences for future faculty and student recruitment efforts. These changes deserve in-depth analysis for MU to return to its roots. . . .

The leadership style of the new management at MU seems to be a primary point of friction. Leadership style, using Hersey-Blanchard's Situational Leadership Model (1988), depends on primarily three factors: follower readiness, relationship behavior, and task behavior. At MU, the culture that was created by previous leadership made the faculty and staff "able and willing" to do their jobs and fulfill the university's mission, demonstrating that they had high follower readiness (Konopaske et al., 2018, p. 416). In such a situation, Hersey-Blanchard's model predicts an appropriate leadership style would have low task behavior, either leaving much of the direction of the faculty and staff to themselves or sharing in governance of the institution. In contrast, the new leadership at MU seems to have adopted a Telling Leadership style, with high task behavior and low relationship behavior. This style has been shown in the institution of monthly performance reviews and the proliferation of new and detailed policies and procedures at every level of the organization. The mismatch between the high readiness of the employees and the high task behavior of the leadership creates a tension between management and labor while also doing damage to the culture of high achievement that had already been established.

The lack of diversity of the leadership team is another concern . . .

Finally, the new leadership has raised the prospect of organizational culture clash through shifting the priorities of the university. . . .

This leadership-directed change in the culture has impacted the motivation and retention of MU's highly accomplished and diverse culture . . .

Text 3 is structured with an evaluative claim about leadership—a theme that emerged from the case—and several supporting claims that use related organizational behavior concepts to present and organize the information in the subsequent paragraphs by making evaluative claims in the topic sentences. In the full paragraph shown and annotated in Figure 1.4, we can see that the claim merges information from the disciplinary theory (*leadership style*) and the case (*new leadership at MU being a point of friction*). The paragraph proceeds with an elaboration of disciplinary knowledge about leadership style (*Leadership style, using Hersey-Blanchard's Situational Leadership Model (1988) depends on . . .*) that will be used to analyze the case. The analysis of M University is supported by details from the case (*At MU, the culture that was created by previous leadership made the faculty and staff*) with further connections to disciplinary knowledge (*In such a situation, Hersey-Blanchard's model predicts an appropriate leadership style*) in an effort to build an argument supported by an analysis of the case applying disciplinary knowledge.

Figure 1.4: Annotated Paragraph From Mentor Case Analysis

The leadership style of the new management at MU seems to be a primary point of friction.	**Argument 1** *Uses disciplinary vocabulary to name claim
Leadership style, using Hersey-Blanchard's Situational Leadership Model (1988), depends on primarily three factors: follower readiness, relationship behavior, and task behavior.	*Anchors analysis in disciplinary knowledge
At MU, the culture that was created by previous leadership made the faculty and staff "able and willing" to do their jobs and fulfill the university's mission, demonstrating that they had high follower readiness (Konopaske et al., 2018, p. 416).	*Provides details from the case
In such a situation, Hersey-Blanchard's model predicts an appropriate leadership style would have low task behavior, either leaving much of the direction of the faculty and staff to themselves or sharing in governance of the institution.	*Elaborates using disciplinary knowledge
In contrast, the new leadership at MU seems to have adopted a Telling Leadership style, with high task behavior and low relationship behavior.	*Provides details from the case
This style has been shown in the institution of monthly performance reviews and the proliferation of new and detailed policies and procedures at every level of the organization.	*Provides details from the case as evidence
The mismatch between the high readiness of the employees and the high task behavior of the leadership creates a tension between management and labor while also doing damage to the culture of high achievement that had already been established.	*Brings paragraph to closure by reiterating claim and stating wider implications

The importance of ideational meanings in the Case Analysis genre is evident when students write an ineffective Case Analysis. One of the most common challenges students face when writing a Case Analysis genre is applying a disciplinary framework to analyze the case. Instead, students report on the disciplinary knowledge acquired in class or report on the case information. Some students ignore the invitation to use disciplinary knowledge to make an overarching claim about the case that needs to be supported with arguments that effectively manage authoritative voices from the discipline and case information. Thus, the ideational resources of the 3x3 are key to helping students engage in analytical work, as discussed in Chapters 2, 3, and 4.

6. Applying the 3x3 to Scaffold First-Year Writing

Our work scaffolding arguments in history and the Case Analysis genre led us to reconceptualize how we teach argument in our first-year writing courses and the kinds of assignments that best prepare students for writing in the disciplines. Our first-year writing courses are theme-based, and the theme of the course becomes the disciplinary knowledge that the students use to analyze a case of their choice. One of the changes that we made in our first-year writing courses was to include a Problem Analysis assignment that prepares students to use the language resources that are important for writing case analyses in their disciplinary courses. While students are expected to propose some potential ways to solve the problems identified in their analysis, the pedagogical focus is on their argument about a problem. This focus is similar to what is expected in the first- and second-year disciplinary classes at our university (Pessoa et al., 2020). The students are expected to write an argument that follows the stages of the Case Analysis genre: Background (an introduction to the case that leads to a problem related to the course's theme), Thesis (main claim and preview of supporting claims about the problem represented by the case), supporting claims (supported by the application of the disciplinary framework to details of the case), and Reinforcement (reaffirming and strengthening the Thesis).

For example, Text 4 shows an annotated introduction and an argument stage of a mentor text to scaffold the Problem Analysis assignment in one first-year writing course where the theme was inequality. In this course, the students learned about the theme by reading authors that discussed inequality using Bourdieu's economic, cultural, and social capital perspective. Text 4 draws on key concepts from these readings to analyze the case of the inequalities associated with the Chilean University Selection Test (or PSU in Spanish).

TEXT 4: Abridged Mentor Text to Scaffold a Problem Analysis Assignment in a First-Year Writing Course

My niece who lives in Chile is about to graduate high school and she has her choice of several top universities where she will pursue a track to be a medical doctor. But she is one of the lucky ones; she is a good test taker and, more importantly, her family was able to afford to send her to private school and even get her a tutor to prepare for the entrance exams.	**Background Stage:** *Introduces case study with shared context: a personal story that relates to the case
Many Chilean students, however, will never get such a chance. The scores Chilean students earn on the University Selection Test (or PSU in Spanish) determine where, and even *if*, they will be able to continue their education after high school. The unfairness of this situation has been recently brought to light by student protesters who disrupted the PSU testing days by blocking the entrances to the exam.	*Introduces the problem; broadens the perspective from one case to a larger social problem
These protests have occurred largely because students who attend private schools are much more likely to qualify for college study than students who attend public schools.	*Provides contextual details about the case
Thus, the Chilean educational system is contributing to the reproduction of economic inequality in ways that are harmful to society.	**Thesis Stage:** *States Main Claim
Whereas the PSU might seem like an equalizer, a standardized test to determine the merit of individuals, such a view obscures the role of cultural capital in student achievement and gives an advantage to the wealthy.	*Previews Supporting Claim 1
The children of parents with strong social capital may be able to switch academic tracks once they are admitted, whereas students who lack these connections are locked into their career path.	*Previews Supporting Claim 2
If steps are not taken to reform the education system, Chile will remain on a dangerous path towards a society that creates opportunities mostly for the wealthy.	*Explains significance of the Thesis
Standardized tests like the PSU give the appearance of providing every student an equal chance to show their merit while favoring those whose parents can afford to cultivate their cultural capital.	**Supporting Claim 1**
Sociologist Shamus Khan (2011), in his study of elite US high school students, explains how the perceived fairness of a meritocracy makes "differences in outcomes appear a product of who people are rather than a product of the conditions of their making" (p. 9).	*Manages external voice (from course reading) to develop points

This exact idea applies to the case of Chile, the country with the highest level of inequality in Latin America (Latin American Index, 2019). In Chile, only 30% of public-school students score high enough on the PSU to qualify for college, compared to around 80% of private school students (Nugent, 2020). And of those who go to private schooling, 80% pay for special classes after school to prepare for the PSU (Salazar, 2019).	*Elaborates evidence
Such statistics reinforce Khan's claim that "there is nothing innate about merit" (p. 6), and indicate that while the test may be standardized, the accessibility of cultural capital needed to succeed is not, as valued forms of cultural capital are closely tied to income (Lareau 2002).	*Manages external voices (from course readings) to show how the evidence supports the claim
Whereas the PSU might seem like an equalizer, a standardized test to determine the merit of individuals, such a view obscures the role of cultural capital in student achievement and gives an advantage to the wealthy	*Concedes by acknowledging potential opposing view and then countering to align the reader
Equal access to quality education is vital to reversing worldwide trends of economic inequality (Alvaredo et al., 2019), but clearly in Chile such access is not currently provided. This type of system reproduces inequality across generations, limiting education's power to enable social mobility for those who can't "afford" merit.	*Brings paragraph to closure by reiterating claim and stating wider implications

In Text 4, ideational meanings take prominence as the student is expected to draw on the disciplinary framework of Bourdieu's capital and key concepts from the readings on inequality through nominalizations that condense information. These key concepts are used to present the main claim (thesis) and supporting claims of the text and to organize the information. Thus, the thesis and the supporting claims include key words from the course readings (*reproduction of economic inequality*, *merit*, *cultural capital*, *social capital*) to make claims at the beginning of the body paragraphs. The use of disciplinary key words to make claims is presented in Chapter 3.

While managing external voices to support the argument is important in Case Analysis writing, controlling ideational meanings by using disciplinary knowledge to present and organize information is vital to meeting expectations for this genre. We discuss ideational resources in depth in Chapter 4.

7. How to Use the 3x3 to Scaffold Argumentative Writing

While we have used the 3x3 extensively to identify the salient features of an expected genre, analyze student writing, diagnose student problems with argumentative writing, and design materials to scaffold argumentative writing, we do not use the 3x3 with our students because it can be overwhelming. Instead, we design materials based on the 3x3 to tackle specific expectations depending on the kinds of argumentative texts students are asked to write. We showcase these materials throughout the book. We have also developed writing assessment rubrics that are based on the 3x3. Chapter 7 provides examples of these rubrics.

8. The Teaching and Learning Cycle

Framed within SFL-genre pedagogy, our approach to scaffolding writing uses elements of the Teaching and Learning Cycle (TLC) (Rothery, 1996). The TLC is an interactive and iterative writing-focused pedagogical cycle of teaching and learning activities. After building content knowledge in a course, the TLC moves through three core stages: deconstruction, joint construction, and independent construction of text. In the deconstruction phase, the teacher engages students in analyzing a mentor text's purpose, stages, and language. In joint construction, students practice writing the target genre with their teacher in preparation for independent construction. Then, once ready, the students write independently. This process is described as "guidance through interaction in the context of shared experience" (Martin, 1999, p. 126). If students are not ready, further cycles of deconstruction and joint construction can be undertaken, with smaller groups of students.

Much of our scaffolding efforts focus on deconstructing sample texts with students. We often compare less successful texts with mentor texts to unpack the valued features of argumentative texts and help students see the effect on the reader when these features are missing or underdeveloped. Due to time constraints and the length of the writing that university students produce, in our work, we often do not engage students in joint construction. Instead, during the independent construction stage, we include further support through cycles of drafting, feedback, and negotiated construction. In negotiated construction, we use drafts of student writing and workshop them individually with students or during whole-class discussions. Our research shows that the inclusion of cycles of feedback and negotiated construction within independent construction is particularly important as explicit instruction through the deconstruction of texts may not be enough for students to meet genre expectations. In higher education, negotiated construction after the teacher has provided feedback on students' first drafts may be more feasible and beneficial than joint construction. In negotiated construction, the students work with their own texts, which is likely to generate more investment from the students (Gómez-Laich et al., 2023). Many of the lessons highlighted in this book involve activities that engage students in deconstruction and negotiated construction of texts to make genre expectations explicit and enhance independent construction.

References

Brisk, M. E. (2022). *Engaging students in academic literacies: SFL genre pedagogy for K-8 classrooms*. Routledge.

Coffin, C. (2006). *Historical discourse: The language of time, cause and evaluation*. Continuum.

Dreyfus, S., Humphrey, S., Mahboob, A., & Martin, J. M. (2016). *Genre pedagogy in higher education. The SLATE project*. Palgrave Macmillan.

Feez, S. (2002). Heritage and innovation in second language education. In A. M. Johns (Ed.), *Genre in the classroom: Multiple perspectives* (pp. 43–69). Lawrence Erlbaum Associates.

Gómez-Laich, M. P., Pessoa, S., & Mahboob, A. (2023). Writing development of the case analysis genre: The importance of feedback and negotiated construction in the Teaching Learning Cycle. In D. Zhang, & R. T. Miller (Eds.), *Crossing boundaries in researching, understanding, and improving language education: Essays in honor of G. Richard Tucker* (pp. 169–188). Springer.

Halliday, M. A. K. (1985). *An introduction to functional grammar*. Edward Arnold.

Halliday, M. A. K. (1994). *An introduction to functional grammar*. Edward Arnold.

Halliday, M. A. K. (2007). *Language and society*. Continuum.

Halliday, M. A. K., & Matthiessen, C. M. I. (2004). *An introduction to functional grammar*. Routledge.

Humphrey, S. (2013). And the word became text: A 4x4 toolkit for scaffolding writing in secondary English. *English in Australia*, *48*, 46–55.

Humphrey, S. L., & Economou, D. (2015). Peeling the onion–A textual model of critical analysis. *Journal of English for Academic Purposes*, *17*, 37–50.

Humphrey, S., Martin, J. R., Dreyfus, S., & Mahboob, A. (2010). The 3x3: Setting up a linguistic toolkit for teaching academic writing. In A. Mahboob, & N. K. Knight (Eds.), *Appliable linguistics* (pp. 185–199). Continuum.

Martin, J. R. (1992). *English text: System and structure*. John Benjamins.

Martin, J. R. (1999). Mentoring semogenesis: 'Genre-based' literacy pedagogy. In F. Christie (Ed.), *Pedagogy and the shaping of consciousness: Linguistic and social processes,* (pp. 123–155). Cassell (Open Linguistics Series).

Martin, J. R., & Rose, D. (2008). *Genre relations: Mapping culture*. Equinox.

Miller, R. T., Mitchell, T. D., & Pessoa, S. (2014). Valued voices: Students' use of Engagement in argumentative history writing. *Linguistics and Education*, *28,* 107–120.

Miller, R. T., Mitchell, T. D., & Pessoa, S. (2016). Impact of source texts and prompts on students' genre uptake. *Journal of Second Language Writing, 31,* 11–24.

Mitchell, T. D. & Pessoa, S. (2017). Scaffolding the writing development of the argument genre in history: The case of two novice writers. *Journal of English for Academic Purposes, 30,* 26–37.

Pessoa, S., Gómez-Laich, M. P., & Mitchell, T. D. (2020). Mapping the case analysis genre continuum in an Information Systems program. *Journal of Writing Research*, *12*, 291–320.

Pessoa, S., Gómez-Laich, M. P., Liginlal, D., & Mitchell, T. D. (2019). Scaffolding case analysis writing: A collaboration between Information Systems and Writing Faculty. *Journal of Information Systems Education*, *30*(1), 42–56.

Pessoa, S., Mitchell, T. D., & Miller, R. T. (2017). Emergent arguments: A functional approach to analyzing student challenges with the argument genre. *Journal of Second Language Writing*, *38*, 42–55.

Pessoa, S., Mitchell, T. D., Gómez-Laich, M. P, Maune, M., & Le Roux, C. (2022). Scaffolding the case analysis in an organizational behavior course: Making analytical language explicit. *Journal of Management Education*, *46*, 226–251.

Rose, D., & Martin, J. R. (2012). *Learning to write, reading to learn: Genre, knowledge and pedagogy in the Sydney School*. Equinox Publishing Ltd.

Rothery, J. (1996). Making changes: Developing an educational linguistics. In R. Hasan & G. Williams (Eds.), *Literacy in society* (pp. 86–123). Longman.

Schleppegrell, M. J. (2004). *The language of schooling: A functional linguistics perspective*. Lawrence Erlbaum.

CHAPTER 2

The Onion Model: A Resource to Help Students Move From Knowledge Display to Knowledge Transformation

1. What Is the Expectation and What Is the Challenge for Students?

Meeting the genre expectations of university writing assignments can pose several challenges for students. Our research (Miller et al., 2016; Mitchell et al., 2021) shows that students often struggle with the analytical expectations of writing assignments, engaging primarily in *knowledge display* by demonstrating their understanding of a reading, a case, or disciplinary knowledge rather than engaging in the higher-level skill of *knowledge transformation* (Scardamalia & Bereiter, 1987) by using disciplinary knowledge as a lens to identify and analyze problems in, for example, a case.

How do writers move from knowledge display to knowledge transformation? And how can teachers help their students engage in knowledge transformation? In this chapter, we present the Onion Model, a model of academic writing development proposed by Humphrey and Economou (2015), as a resource to help students move from knowledge display to knowledge transformation.

2. What Does the Challenge Look Like in First-Year Writing and in Writing in the Disciplines?

Over the years at our institution, many assignments in the first-year writing courses have asked students to engage in knowledge transformation by analyzing a text or a case. For example, in one course students were required to read a lengthy and complex academic argument and write an Argument Analysis. The students had to break the argument down into parts and then put it back together in their own way. Rather than re-presenting the author's argument according to the chronology of the source text, the students had to find connections between different parts of the argument. They had to identify the author's most important supporting claims and figure out how evidence presented in the different parts of the text worked together to bolster those claims. However, instead of doing this analytical work, many students summarized the text's content in its original order.

In this same class, at the end of the semester students were asked to write an analysis of a case informed by the concepts from the course readings, all of which focused on the relationship between urban planning and society. In this assignment, the students had to choose a place (e.g., a shopping mall, their own neighborhood) and a social phenomenon (e.g., fast urban development) in a city they were familiar with. They had to use course concepts to support an argument about this place, "contributing to" the academic conversation on urban planning and society that they had read about all semester. However, some students described the case without connecting it to the literature read and discussed in class.

In these examples, students engaged in knowledge display rather than knowledge transformation, thus failing to meet the genre expectations of engaging in analysis and argument.

Similar challenges arise in student responses to disciplinary writing assignments. In information systems, business administration, and management programs, students are often asked to write a Case Analysis. A Case Analysis is a written response that includes an analysis of an organization, using disciplinary concepts to identify problems or opportunities in the case, followed by recommendations for enhancing the organization's practices. For example, in an information systems course at our institution, students were asked to analyze the company LEGO and identify its strategic value through the lens of Porter's Five Forces (Porter, 1985). In an organizational behavior course, students analyzed the grocery store Whole Foods after it was acquired by Amazon, identified problems and opportunities at Whole Foods related to key organizational behavior concepts (e.g., leadership, culture, or employee motivation), and argued for a recommendation to address the problems identified in the analysis.

In our work scaffolding Case Analysis writing in these disciplines, we have found that students struggle to meet genre expectations because they engage in knowledge display rather than in knowledge transformation. The students often describe the case or report information from the textbook and fail to engage in knowledge transformation by applying disciplinary knowledge to identify problems within the case.

3. What Resource Can We Use to Address the Problem?

To help students move from knowledge display to knowledge transformation, we use the Onion Model, a model of academic writing development proposed by Humphrey and Economou (2015). This model is used to refer to the relationship between four different discourse patterns that are valued across academic disciplines: description, analysis, argument, and critique. These discourse patterns are layered and interdependent.

Description involves the reproduction of knowledge by summarizing, presenting a list of facts, or recounting a series of events or activities:

> *Whole Foods is an American multinational supermarket that has over 500 branches in the U.S. Whole Foods was founded in 1980. In 2017, Whole Foods was acquired by Amazon.*

Analysis requires the reorganization of information in some original way for the purposes of the text and often involves the application of a disciplinary framework to an exemplar. A disciplinary framework may be thought of as a discipline's agreed-upon classificatory and compositional schemes or, in other words, its analytical lenses. Table 2.1 shows examples of disciplinary frameworks.

Table 2.1: Examples of Disciplinary Frameworks

Discipline	Disciplinary frameworks	Elements of the frameworks
English	Toulmin's argument model	Claims, reasons, warrants, rebuttal, backing
	Stasis theory	Existence, definition, value, cause, action
History	Processes of historical change	Change and continuity; gradual and sudden changes; political, economic, social, and cultural changes
	Explanation of historical events	Multiple causes, types of causes, relationships between causes, long-term and immediate consequences
Information systems	Innovation	Process, product, disruptive, incremental, complementary, architectural
	Porter's Five Forces	Competitive rivalry, supplier power, buyer power, threat of substitution, threat of new entry
Business administration	Feasibility	Technical, economic, operational/organizational, schedule, legal/cultural
Organizational behavior	Situational leadership model	Directing, coaching, supporting, delegating
	Organizational change	Freezing, moving, refreezing
Sociology	Capital	Social, economic, cultural, linguistic
	Assimilation	Upward, downward, segmented
Psychology	Psychoanalysis	Transference, repetition compulsion, fixation, cathexis, regression, identification with the aggressor, and loss of possession of self
	Positive organizational psychology	Positive individual attributes, positive emotions, strengths and virtues, positive relationships, positive human resource practices, positive organizational processes, positive leadership, and change
Biology	Life	Kingdom, phylum, class, order, family, genus, species
	Mechanisms of fungal disease	Recognized mechanisms (infection, allergy, toxicity) and contested mechanisms (presence of any mold)
Physics	Matter	Quarks, leptons, gluon, photon
Design	Visual design elements	Font, color, visual hierarchy, symbols, alignment, proximity
	User experience	Useful, usable, desirable

In an English writing class, students may be asked to use stasis theory to identify where different authors' positions on an issue align with and depart from each other. History students may be asked to analyze the causes of the French Revolution using a cause-and-effect framework to consider overlapping causes. Design students may be asked to analyze a poster by considering the author's use of design elements like color and symbols to achieve a communicative effect. What is common among these examples is that the student needs to determine how details from the object of analysis relate to distinct elements of the disciplinary framework.

When writers engage in analysis, they break down a complex text or situation (such as the case of the LEGO company) into smaller parts and show how the complex information fits into the elements of the disciplinary framework. The disciplinary framework is then used to present and organize the text. This type of organization and the corresponding work of parsing the source material is what makes this text analytical rather than descriptive (see sample texts in the next section).

The Argument genre involves the representation of an explicit evaluation, which typically unfolds with a text organized by a claim and reasons. Arguments use both descriptive and analytical language, but in the service of an overarching explicit evaluation that is usually made at the beginning of a text and is supported throughout the text using reasons. In the example of the LEGO Case Analysis, the evaluation would be whether, for example, the threat of substitute products is high, moderate, or low for LEGO, and the reasons would be supported with analysis that incorporates description: the student would need to analyze LEGO using the disciplinary framework of Porter's Five Forces (Porter, 1985) and blend description of an example with analysis of what has been described. The key point here is that description is used in the service of the analysis, and both description and analysis are used in the service of the main argument of the text.

Finally, critique involves challenging an established authorial opinion and persuading the reader to accept an alternative/counter position. Since much of undergraduate writing does not focus on critiquing, in our work to help students move from knowledge display to knowledge transformation we have focused on unpacking the language of description, analysis, and argument.

4. Lessons

4.1. Moving From Knowledge Display to Knowledge Transformation Using Sample Texts

We suggest using sample texts to help students identify the different patterns of academic writing (i.e., description, analysis, and argument).

The Onion Model

Below, we include three excerpts of texts from the discipline of information systems: a descriptive text, an analytical text, and an argumentative text. The three sample texts are based on responses to Case Analysis assignments assigned in a first-year information systems course. The first two texts use the disciplinary framework of Porter's Five Forces, and the third text uses the disciplinary framework of Innovation.

SAMPLE 1: Porter's Five Forces: Descriptive Text

Porter's Five Forces is a framework for assessing the sources of competition in an industry or business. Understanding those sources of competition is important for a business to adjust its strategy, increase profitability and stay ahead of the competition. Porter identified five forces to measure competition: **competitive rivalry, threat of new entrants, buyer power, supplier power,** and **the threat of substitutes. Competitive rivalry** refers to the number and capability of competitors in the market. The larger the number of competitors who offer similar services and products, the lesser the power of a company. The **threat of new entrants** refers to the possibility and likelihood of new companies entering an industry and eroding profitability. Two other forces are **buyer power** and **supplier power. Buyer power** refers to the buyers' ability to manipulate the industry and drive prices down. If a business has few powerful buyers, they are often able to negotiate for lower prices and better deals. On the contrary, **supplier power** refers to how easy it is for suppliers to drive up prices. The fewer suppliers an industry has, the more a company will depend on a supplier. As a result, the supplier has more power to drive up input costs. The last of Porter's Five Forces is **the threat of substitutes.** Substitute goods or services pose a threat to a company. When close substitute products are available in the market, customers can switch to those alternative products and reduce a company's power. On the contrary, companies that produce goods or services for which there are no close substitutes have more power to increase prices.

When LEGO was founded in 1932, there were not many competitors in the market. LEGO was the first company to manufacture interlocking bricks for children to play with and develop their fine motor skills. Recently, several companies have started manufacturing similar products and competition has therefore increased.

SAMPLE 2: Porter's Five Forces: Analytical Text

Porter's Five Forces is a framework for assessing the sources of competition in an industry or business. Understanding those sources of competition is important for a business to adjust its strategy, increase profitability and stay ahead of the competition. Porter identified five forces to measure competition: **competitive rivalry, threat of new**

entrants, buyer power, supplier power, and the threat of substitutes. Of these, the most relevant for LEGO are competitive rivalry and the threat of substitute products.

For LEGO, competitive rivalry comes from the number of competitors in the market. Competitive rivalry refers to the number and capability of competitors in the market. Over the years, several toy manufacturing companies have been established and their products have had wide acceptability in the market. However, customers' loyalty has helped LEGO mitigate this rivalry. In fact, brand loyalty has made it tough for the new toy manufacturing companies to draw customers away from LEGO.

Naturally, due to the existence of competitors in the industry, LEGO has also paid particular attention to the threat of substitute products. This threat refers to substitute goods or services that pose a threat to a company. This threat comes from the products that rivals make. The biggest threat to LEGO comes from rival clone brands that make blocks that are compatible with LEGO's bricks, and which advertise themselves as "compatible with leading building bricks." One of these is COBI, a Polish brand founded in 1987 that offers a huge selection of brick toy themes such as their World of Tanks line and their Small Army line. Another threat for LEGO is Oxford, a South-Korean brick toy manufacturer founded in 1961 that offers a variety of sets with several themes, including military, transport, and police. Oxford also has licenses to make theme-based sets from Disney and Hello Kitty. To mitigate the threat of substitute products, LEGO has adopted a strategy of differentiation from its competitors: it has adapted its products to consumers' wants and it has diversified its products through innovative, physical-digital integration into play.

SAMPLE 3: Innovation: Argumentative Text

LEGO was successful in its approach to innovation, particularly in its use of complementary and incremental innovation.

LEGO's use of complementary innovation was successful because it led to an increase in profits and to the growth of the company's customer base. Complementary innovation is the process of creating new products that "complement" a company's existing products to enhance the original product. One of the innovations that LEGO implemented that helped to increase its profit was obtaining licensing agreements to complement its products by producing Star Wars characters. According to Professor McNally (2015), since obtaining this licensing arrangement, LEGO has sold over 200 million Star Wars LEGO boxes and "LEGO Star Wars continues to rank among the best-selling global toy lines" (p. 250). This shows the great success of this complementary innovation initiative. Another example of a complementary product that was a success is Bionicle, a line of LEGO construction toys that has become one of

The Onion Model   31

the company's biggest-selling properties. Although some of the early complementary products that LEGO produced did not sell well (i.e., Znap), the majority of LEGO's later complementary products were well-received by the public. This shows that LEGO was successful in the use of complementary innovation as it increased the company' profits.

LEGO's use of complementary innovation was also successful because it led to an increase in the number of customers . . .

LEGO was also successful in its use of incremental innovation . . .

Without telling the students whether each text is descriptive, analytical, or argumentative, engage students in analyzing the texts for the differences between description, analysis, and argument. You can use guiding questions such as the following:

1. How is the text organized?
2. What is the focus of each paragraph?
3. How do the paragraphs relate to each other?
4. What are some of the language choices that tell you about the text's structure?
5. Can you identify a disciplinary framework? What is it and how it is used in the text?
6. What language reveals that the writer is analyzing and not describing?

Show students how, in Sample 1, the writer presents information as factual, interpreting the assignment as an invitation to display knowledge of the disciplinary framework and the details of the case, rather than transform knowledge for the purposes of the text. In paragraph 1, the writer identifies and defines each of the five forces to measure competition, displaying agreed-upon knowledge from the discipline and organizing the information by entities (e.g., *Porter's Five Forces is a framework for assessing the sources of competition in an industry or business. Competitive rivalry refers to . . . . The threat of new entrants refers to . . . . Two other forces are buyer power and supplier power. Buyer power refers to . . . . On the contrary, supplier power refers to . . . . The last of Porter's Five Forces is the threat of substitutes . . .*). Use the visualization in Figure 2.1 to show this text annotated for its descriptive language.

Figure 2.1: Text Annotated for Its Descriptive Features

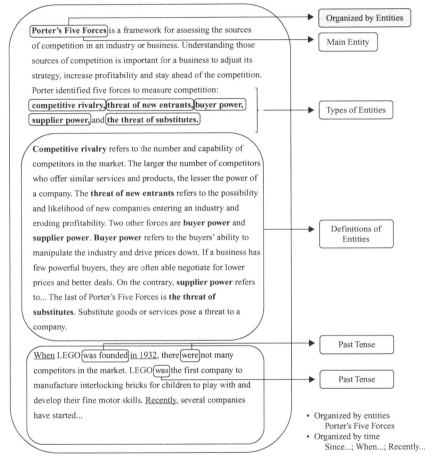

Move to Sample 2, the analytical text. Tell students that this text is based on a Case Analysis assignment that asked students to respond to this prompt: *Analyze the LEGO case using Porter's Five Forces framework. What forces has LEGO focused on to stay ahead of the competition? Use the information provided in the case and other available information about the related industry.* Emphasize how, in order to respond effectively, the writer had to engage in analytical work using the disciplinary framework of Porter's Five Forces. The writer had to read the source texts related to the LEGO case, break down the case of LEGO into its parts and group them according to *relevant* elements of the disciplinary framework of Porter's Five Forces (competitive rivalry, threat of new entrants, buyer power, supplier power, and the threat of substitutes). While there are five elements in

The Onion Model

the disciplinary framework of Porter's Five Forces, the student determined that the competitive rivalry and threat of substitute products were most relevant to understanding LEGO's competitive strategy and uses these relevant elements of the disciplinary framework to present and organize the ideas. The student focuses on competitive rivalry in paragraph 1 and on the threat of substitute products in paragraph 2. These elements of the disciplinary framework are presented as abstract nouns, fronted in the topic sentences, and defined before the writer unpacks them with details from the case in the paragraphs. This type of organization is what makes this text analytical rather than descriptive. Figure 2.2 shows this text annotated for these features.

Figure 2.2: Text Annotated for Its Analytical Features

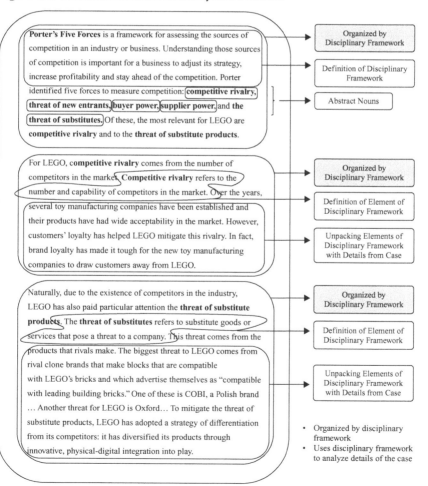

Move to Sample 3, the argumentative text. Tell students this argumentative text is a response to a prompt that asked students to evaluate how successful LEGO was in implementing innovation. Emphasize how, to respond effectively, the writer had to engage in analytical and argumentative work using the disciplinary framework of Innovation. Ask students how this text differs from the analytical one. Emphasize that the argumentative text is organized using a claim-reasons framework that integrates the disciplinary framework-based analysis as support for an evaluation; the text fronts an evaluative claim (*LEGO was successful in its approach to innovation*) and then provides reasons for this claim (e.g., *LEGO's use of complementary innovation was successful because*). The writer uses abstract nouns to categorize details of the case that support the evaluation (e.g., *increase in profits, the growth of the company's customer base*, and *increase in the number of customers*) before unpacking them as a concrete description that functions as evidence (*One of the innovations that LEGO implemented . . . was obtaining . . .*). The writer uses interpersonal resources, indicating an awareness of a reader who needs to be aligned to the position taken in these evaluations. The writer integrates outside voices from the case's source texts and other outside sources strategically (e.g., *According to Professor McNally (2015), . . .*). The writer then shows how the evidence presented supports the claims and reasons (e.g., *this shows that, this confirms that*). The writer also uses interpersonal resources to show that a reader's potential reactions have been anticipated and potential objections have been countered with more evidence (e.g., <u>*Although*</u> *some of the early complementary products that LEGO produced did not sell well (i.e., Znap),* <u>*the majority of*</u> *LEGO's later complementary products were well-received by the public.*). Figure 2.3 shows this text annotated for these features.

The Onion Model

Figure 2.3: Text Annotated for Its Argumentative Features

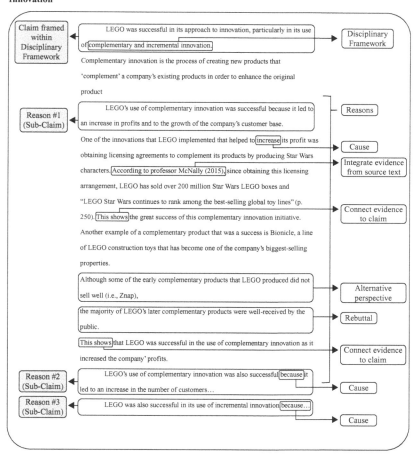

Below, we include two sample texts from a first-year sample Problem Analysis: a descriptive text and an argumentative text. In these Problem Analysis assignments, students had to select a case related to inequality (i.e., the topic of the course) and analyze it through the lens of Pierre Bourdieu's concept of capital and other relevant course concepts (the course's analytical framework). We defined a case as a story of a person the students know, a group of people, or a community; a current event; or a social phenomenon that points to a problem related to unequal access economic, cultural, and/or social capital that contributes to social class reproduction and, ultimately, inequality.

SAMPLE 1: SATs in Chile (Sample Problem Analysis): Descriptive Text

STUDENT PROTESTS IN CHILE: A SYMPTOM OF DEMOCRATIC INEQUALITY

Introduction:

My niece who lives in Chile is about to graduate high school and she has her choice of several top universities where she will pursue a track to be a medical doctor. But she is one of the lucky ones; she is a good test taker and, more importantly, her family was able to afford sending her to private school and even getting her a tutor to prepare for the entrance exams. Many Chilean students, however, will never get such a chance. The score Chilean students earn on the University Selection Test (or PSU in Spanish), the standardized test used for college admissions in Chile, determines where, and even *if*, they will be able to continue their education after high school. This situation has been recently brought to light by student protesters who disrupted the PSU testing days by blocking the entrances to the exam. These protests have occurred largely because students who attend private schools are over two and a half times as likely to qualify for college study than students who attend public schools, with only 30% of public-school students qualifying for college study (Nugent, 2020).

Sample Body Paragraph:

The Chilean PSU, a standardized national test used for college admissions in Chile, is taken by over 300,000 students every year and it is similar to the SAT or ACT in the United States. The score students get on this test determines where, and even *if*, they will be able to continue their education after high school. In Chile, only 30% of public-school students score high enough on the PSU to qualify for college, compared to around 80% of private school students (Nugent, 2020). Only 6 out of 10 students' parents can afford to pay for private or semi-private schooling (Nugent, 2020). And of those who go to private schools, 80% of them must pay for special classes after school to prepare for the PSU. Clearly, the current system is placing a significant portion of the Chilean population at a disadvantage, greatly contributing to increasing inequality. The Latin American Inequality Index (2019) places Chile as the country with the highest level of inequality in Latin America. Such high levels of inequality have significant negative consequences for access to quality education and ensuring socio-economic mobility.

SAMPLE 2: SATs in Chile (Sample Problem Analysis): Analytical and Argumentative Text

STUDENT PROTESTS IN CHILE: A SYMPTOM OF DEMOCRATIC INEQUALITY

Introduction:

My niece who lives in Chile is about to graduate high school and she has her choice of several top universities where she will pursue a track to be a medical doctor. But she is one of the lucky ones; she is a good test taker and, more importantly, her family was able to afford sending her to private school and even getting her a tutor to prepare for the entrance exams. Many Chilean students, however, will never get such a chance. The scores Chilean students earn on the University Selection Test (or PSU in Spanish) determine where, and even *if*, they will be able to continue their education after high school. The unfairness of this situation has been recently brought to light by student protesters who disrupted the PSU testing days by blocking the entrances to the exam.

These protests have occurred largely because students who attend private schools are over two and a half times as likely to qualify for college study than students who attend public schools, with only 30% of public-school students qualifying for college study (Nugent, 2020). Chilean society does not provide all students with equal access to adequate preparation for the test and harms many students' life chances to pursue careers that will advance their economic position. Thus, the Chilean educational system, where privatization has created unequal access to education, is contributing to the reproduction of economic inequality in ways that are harmful to society. Whereas the PSU might seem like an equalizer, a single test to determine the merit of individuals, such a view obscures the fact that the society promotes "democratic inequality" in the guise of meritocracy (Khan, 2011). Since parents who have limited economic mobility are often unable to provide their children with chances to gain cultural capital necessary for themselves to become upwardly mobile, inequality in Chile is likely to persist. Equal access to quality education is vital to reversing worldwide trends of economic inequality, but clearly in Chile such access is not currently provided (Alvaredo et al., 2018). Since giving everyone a fair chance to earn what they merit is a widely shared value, countries such as Chile need to re-examine their educational policies or events like the student protests of 2020 are likely to get worse.

Sample Body Paragraph:

The Chilean student protests are symptoms of inequality caused by the PSU being a "false equalizer." In other words, the exam gives the impression of creating fairness, a beneficial tool of meritocracy, when in fact it is a problematic tool that reproduces economic inequality. Khan (2011) is highly critical of the idea of meritocracy, blaming it for the "democratic inequality" that makes society seem more open for more diverse groups even as it becomes more economically unequal: "[the] meritocracy of hard work and achievement has naturalized socially constituted distinctions, making differences in outcomes appear a product of who people are rather than a product of the conditions of their making" (p. 9). This exact idea applies to the case of the Chilean PSU, where only 30% of public-school students score high enough to qualify for college, compared to around 80% of private school students (Nugent, 2020). Only 6 out of 10 students' parents can afford to pay for private or semi-private schooling (Nugent, 2020). And of those who go to private schooling, 80% of them must pay for special classes after school to prepare for the PSU. Clearly, the current system is placing a significant portion of the Chilean population at a disadvantage, greatly contributing to increasing inequality. The Latin American Inequality Index (2019) places Chile as the country with the highest level of inequality in Latin America. Such high levels of inequality have significant negative consequences for access to quality education and ensuring socio-economic mobility. If all students are not given an equal chance to be adequately prepared for the PSU, then students' performance on it does not reflect a true meritocracy. According to Khan (2011), meritocracy . . . . The economic inequality in Chile means that the exam scores are more a product of the conditions of students' making than of who they are. This type of educational system reproduces inequality across generations.

Engage students in analyzing the texts for the differences between description, analysis, and argument. You can use the same guiding questions we presented above, and you can also ask the students to identify and underline key words and information from the disciplinary framework and key words from the case (i.e., information about the case gathered by the writer).

Then, show students how, in Sample 1, the writer presents information as factual, interpreting the assignment as an invitation to display knowledge about the details of the case, rather than transform knowledge for the purposes of the text. The writer begins the introduction with a narrative in the form of a personal story (e.g., *My niece who lives in Chile is about to graduate high school and she has her choice of several top universities where she will pursue a track to be a medical doctor*) and then refers to the protests that took place in Chile in January 2020 when several students protested in the streets about the inequality associated with the PSU test (e.g., *This situation has been recently brought to light by student protesters who disrupted the PSU testing* days by blocking the entrances to the exam). The text does not have a clear main argument in the form of a major claim about inequality that needs to be defended.

Show students how the body paragraph does not begin with a claim but with a definition of the PSU (e.g., *The Chilean PSU, a standardized national test used for college admissions in Chile, is taken by over 300,000 students every year and it is similar to the SAT or ACT in the United States*). Although the writer does try to connect the details of the case to the issue of inequality toward the end of the body paragraph (*Clearly, the current system is placing a significant portion of the Chilean population at a disadvantage, greatly contributing to increasing inequality*), the connection is weak, it is not supported with substantial evidence, and there is no connection to the theoretical lens the student was supposed to use to analyze the case.

Then move to Sample 2 and show students how the writer begins the introduction by connecting their personal narrative to the Chilean protests but then includes a clear claim about inequality that needs to be defended: *Thus, the Chilean educational system, where privatization has created unequal access to education, is contributing to the reproduction of economic inequality in ways that are harmful to society*. After this major claim, the writer previews the supporting claims that include key words from the disciplinary framework and from the case (*Whereas the PSU might seem like an equalizer, a single test to determine the merit of individuals, such a view obscures the fact that the society promotes "democratic inequality" in the guise of meritocracy [Khan, 2011]. Since parents who have limited economic mobility are often unable to provide their children with chances to gain cultural capital necessary for themselves to become upwardly mobile, inequality in Chile is likely to persist.*)

In the following paragraph, the writer fronts the first subclaim (*The Chilean student protests are symptoms of inequality caused by the PSU being a "false equalizer." In other words, the exam gives the impression of creating fairness, a beneficial tool of meritocracy, when in fact it is a problematic tool that reproduces economic inequality*), then brings in an author from the course readings to provide further information about the concept of meritocracy, and then provides reasons and evidence to support the claim in the form of details from the case.

4.2. Identifying When an Assignment Calls for Description, Analysis, or Argument

In addition to developing an awareness of the different patterns of academic writing (i.e., description, analysis, and argument), students need to understand that they might encounter writing assignments that have different pedagogical goals that relate to these patterns. In other words, sometimes instructors solicit knowledge display to gauge if students read or understood course material; sometimes instructors have mixed goals, providing prompts that solicit knowledge display and knowledge transformation on the same assignment. Thus, it is equally important to help students identify *when* an assignment calls for description, analysis, or argument. We suggest using an activity (see Table 2.2) that asks students to identify if assignment prompts and short-answer questions from different disciplines invite them to describe, analyze, or argue (the answers are provided in parentheses).

Table 2.2: Analysis of Assignment Prompts

Look at the following prompts and identify if you are being asked to describe, analyze, or argue:

1. According to the author, what happened when the four disease pools started to converge? (description)
2. To what extent can noise be overcome through good communication design? Support your argument with two or more examples of visual communication and analyze their design elements (e.g., symbols, typography, visual hierarchy) to evaluate their effectiveness in overcoming noise. (argument)
3. What went wrong in LEGO's attempt to grow? How did it recover? (description)
4. Analyze the LEGO case using the concept of innovation. What kinds of innovation did LEGO implement? (analysis)
5. What are the characteristics of a good leader? What characteristics of a good leader does Ugly Betty [the main character in a US television show] exhibit in the episode assigned for homework? (analysis)
6. Describe your experience visiting the museum in detail with a focus on the use of, availability, and access to technology. (description)
7. How compelling do you find McNeill's evidence that disease influences culture? (argument)
8. What problems did Air Canada face with their decentralization of the IT Department? What structure was ultimately adopted and why? (description)
9. What were the social classes in Ancient Babylonia? (description)

The Onion Model 41

4.3. Other Activities for Identifying Whether Students Are Being Asked to Describe, Analyze, or Argue

4.3.1. Ask students to bring prompts from their disciplinary classes to identify if they are being asked to display knowledge or transform knowledge and to identify whether they need to describe, analyze, or argue.

4.3.2. Ask students to research the kinds of disciplinary frameworks used in their disciplines and how they are being asked to apply those disciplinary frameworks in their writing assignments.

4.4. Understanding Analysis and Argument Using a Visualization

Once students have become familiar with the Onion Model, you can use the visualization in Figure 2.4 to walk students through the prewriting process of analysis as a foundation for their analysis and argument. Although this activity focuses on the Case Analysis genre, this process applies to any assignment that requires analysis with a disciplinary framework.

You can use the visualization to show students how it is important to consider the assignment questions and source texts about the case provided by the instructor in light of information about the discipline learned in class and from their own research. The information from the course includes the disciplinary framework, which students must relate to the details of the case (the "data") that they gather from the source texts and their research. The visualization illustrates the need to break down a case into its parts and group details according to *relevant* elements of a disciplinary framework; while there may be many elements that constitute a disciplinary framework, the student might find that certain elements do not relate to the details of the case.

While discussing this process with the students, relate it explicitly to the Onion Model. To encourage students to use purposeful description, encourage them to transcribe information or paraphrase concrete details from the case, placing it under the relevant element of the framework. Reinforce the idea of this being an analytical process that can be applied

Figure 2.4: Visual Representation of the Pre-writing Analytical Process

A Process for <u>Planning</u> a Case Analysis

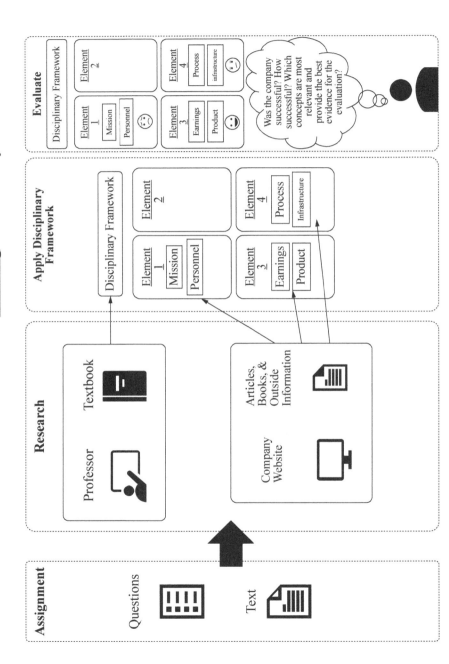

to other assignments or other courses *and* that the same case could be analyzed using a different disciplinary framework.

Although the visualization in Figure 2.4 can be used to raise students' awareness about the prewriting process of analysis in any assignment that asks for analysis using a disciplinary framework, instructors can customize the visualization to make it more relevant to their own assignments. For example, in our first-year writing courses we used the visualization in Figure 2.5 to walk students through the process of planning their Problem Analysis assignment. In this assignment, students select a case related to the topic of the course and analyze it through the lens of the course's theoretical framework. To illustrate, we will refer to the Problem Analysis assignment where students had to select a case related to inequality (i.e., the topic of the course) and analyze it through the lens of Pierre Bourdieu's concept of capital and other relevant course concepts (the course's analytical framework).

As in Figure 2.4, the visualization in Figure 2.5 shows how to break down a case into its parts and group details according to *relevant* elements of a disciplinary framework; while there may be many elements that constitute a disciplinary framework, the student might find that certain elements do not relate to the details of the case. Students then need to use their analysis of the case to argue about the complexities and characteristics of the problem(s) associated with the case or what the case represents. To support their position, they need to draw on details of the case and the course readings. In their writing, students are expected to use Bourdieu's concept of capital and their knowledge about inequality to present and organize information by making claims that use the key words from the expert knowledge they have gained during the course.

You can accompany the visualization with other scaffolding materials to make the process of preparing to write an analytical argument more accessible to the students. For example, in our classes we use two prewriting tasks for the Problem Analysis assignment. The first task scaffolds the "research" and "brainstorm and describe" parts of the process. It asks students to do research on their case and to submit a description of their case together with a list of course readings and other external sources that connect to their case.

Figure 2.5: Visual Representation of the Pre-writing Analytical Process for a Problem Analysis Assignment in a First-year Writing Course

A Process for Planning a Problem Analysis

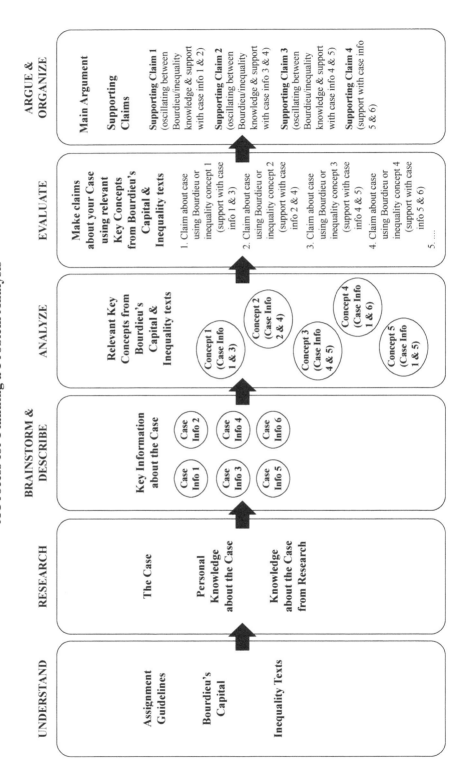

The Onion Model

Case Information and Support for Your Problem Analysis

CASE:

Description of the case: Include background information about your case with plenty of details and how the case represents a problem related to inequality (150–250 words).

Relevant course readings: List in APA style two to three course readings that connect to your case and that you will use to support your argument. Briefly explain how you will use ideas from each text in your problem analysis or include a quote from the text that relates to your case and the argument you are making about your case (approx. 50–75 words per summary).

> APA citation of Source 1:
> Brief explanation or quote:
> APA citation of Source 2:
> Brief explanation or quote:
> APA citation of Source 3:
> Brief explanation or quote:

Other supporting sources: To support your argument, you will need to do some research about your case and the academic conversation it relates to.

You will need to learn more about your case by finding one to two news articles/videos with background information about your case.

You will also need to find one to two journal articles/chapters that will help you support your claims. I recommend starting with the authors we have read this semester, checking what else they have written, who they cite, and/or who cites them. You may also email the librarians for help finding sources.

List the sources you find in APA style and provide a brief explanation on how you will use it in your problem analysis or provide a quote that relates to your case and/or your argument (50–75 words per summary).

One to two news articles/videos with background information about your case:

> APA citation of Source 1:
> Brief explanation or quote:
> APA citation of Source 2:
> Brief explanation or quote:

One to two journal articles/chapters that relate to your case and/or your argument:

> APA citation of Source 1:
> Brief explanation or quote:
> APA citation of Source 2:
> Brief explanation or quote:

The second task scaffolds the "analyze" part of the process. It asks students to brainstorm key words from their case (based on their research on the case) and from the disciplinary framework. We suggest providing students with two or three newspaper articles about a sample case. In our context, we have used the Chilean standardized national test used for college admissions as a sample case. This activity helps students connect the details of the case to the disciplinary framework and group details of the case according to *relevant* elements of a disciplinary framework. Once again, while there may be many elements that constitute the disciplinary framework (i.e., economic capital, cultural capital, social capital), the student might find that certain elements do not relate to the details of the case. You can ask students to complete a chart like the one displayed in Table 2.3.

Table 2.3: Brainstorming Activity for Connecting the Details of the Case to the Disciplinary Framework

	Element of disciplinary framework: economic capital	Element of disciplinary framework: cultural capital	Element of disciplinary framework: social capital
Case information			
Case information			
Case information			
Case information			

Once students have completed these prewriting tasks, they can start thinking about their plan for writing their analytical paragraphs. These paragraphs will be anchored by (supporting) claims, which take shape during the "evaluate" part of the process, and which we discuss in detail in Chapter 3.

5. Concluding Remarks

In this chapter, we presented the Onion Model as a tool that can be used to help students move from knowledge display to knowledge transformation both in their disciplinary courses and in their first-year writing courses. We have also provided suggestions for activities that can help students identify when they are being asked to engage in description, analysis, and argument.

References

Humphrey, S. L., & Economou, D. (2015). Peeling the onion—A textual model of critical analysis. *Journal of English for Academic Purposes*, *17*, 37–50.

Miller, R. T., Mitchell, T. D., & Pessoa, S. (2016). Impact of source texts and prompts on students' genre uptake. *Journal of Second Language Writing, 31*, 11–24.

Mitchell, T. D., Pessoa, S., Gómez-Laich, M. P., & Maune, M. (2021). Degrees of reasoning: Student uptake of a language-focused approach to scaffolding patterns of logical reasoning in the case analysis genre. *TESOL Quarterly, 55*, 1278–1310.

Porter, E. M. (1985). *Competitive Advantage*. The Free Press/Macmillan.

Scardamalia, M., & Bereiter, C. (1987). Knowledge telling and knowledge transforming in written composition. In S. Rosenberg (Ed.), *Cambridge monographs and texts in applied psycholinguistics. Advances in applied psycholinguistics (Vol. 1. Disorders of first-language development; Vol. 2. Reading, writing, and language learning)* (pp. 142–175). Cambridge University Press.

CHAPTER 3

Writing Effective Claims: Key Words, Evaluations, and Causal Relations

1. What Is the Expectation and What Is the Challenge for Students?

Making claims and supporting them with appropriate evidence are key components of argumentative and analytical writing. A claim is a position that a writer takes on a particular issue and is supported by evidence in the form of examples, data, source texts, and logical reasoning. In a typical argumentative text, especially one written for university purposes, the audience expects the writer to make one major claim, called the thesis, at the beginning of the text, and break the thesis down into smaller claims, or supporting claims. Each of these must be supported by evidence. Together, supporting claims build an argument (Coffin, 2006; Wingate, 2012). Table 3.1 shows an example of a thesis and its supporting claims from a history argumentative essay.

Table 3.1: Sample Thesis With Supporting Claims From a History Argument

Prompt: What sort of picture do you get about the status of women in Ancient Babylonia from reading Hammurabi's Code?
Thesis: The main view we get throughout the laws is that women held a much lower status in society than men . . .
Supporting Claim 1: . . . as seen in the derogatory language used in Hammurabi's Code to refer to women, . . .
Supporting Claim 2: . . . they had fewer rights than men in matters such as marriage and divorce.

48

In Chapter 2, we learned about the Onion Model as a tool to help students move from knowledge display to knowledge transformation. We exemplified the process of analysis using a Problem Analysis assignment from our first-year writing courses and we visualized the process of analysis with a diagram that showed what students need to do to be able to analyze a case using disciplinary knowledge. One of the final stages of the process of analysis is for students to make evaluations about the case, which are the basis for the claims in their text.

But how do writers come up with their claims? And how can teachers help their students write effective claims?

To explain paragraphing in argumentative writing, some teachers use the acronym PEEL: Point, Elaboration, Evidence, and Link. PEEL exemplifies how paragraphs start with a point (or claim)—which is then elaborated and supported with evidence—and finish with a link to show how the evidence presented supports the point. However, this approach does not provide concrete strategies for or descriptions of the language resources needed to articulate these elements of a paragraph (Humphrey et al., 2015).

Researchers have described argumentative paragraphs as moving from decontextualized to contextualized and back to decontextualized language (Coffin & Donohue, 2014); from abstract to more concrete language and back to abstract (Dreyfus et al., 2016; Humphrey, 2013; Humphrey et al., 2015; Macnaught et al., 2013); or from principle to example (Duke & Pearson, 2009). Thus, claims are often fronted at the beginning of the paragraph and use abstractions to package information, often as a one-sentence claim that is then developed and supported with concrete evidence in the body of the paragraph. For example, Supporting Claim 1 in Table 3.1 uses the label "derogatory language" to refer to various laws in Hammurabi's Code where women are referred to in pejorative ways in comparison with men. The writer packaged all these negative references to women in the laws with the label "derogatory language."

Our research shows that writing claims is not easy, and students often struggle with writing effective claims. Instead of starting a paragraph in a more abstract way, many students start their paragraphs with an example or a narrative that uses evidence or details from the source text in a more contextualized manner. In other words, students face challenges using abstractions to make a statement that is then unpacked, explained, and supported in the paragraph.

This chapter focuses on how to help students write effective claims.

2. What Does the Challenge Look Like in First-Year Writing and in Writing in the Disciplines?

Table 3.2 shows examples of paragraph starters from argumentative assignments in a first-year writing course and an organizational behavior course. On the left side we show examples of paragraph starters that students often write without explicit instruction, and on the right side we show paragraph starters written after students are explicitly taught how to start an analytical and argumentative paragraph with an effective claim.

Table 3.2: Examples of Claims Without and With Explicit Instruction

Without explicit instruction	With explicit instruction
1a. **For example, Tara** who came from a working-class family didn't know how to write her personal statement for college or who to ask for recommendations and missed the college application deadline.	1b. Students with limited **economic capital** lack **formal or informal knowledge** about the college application process.
2a. **According to Bourdieu (1985),** "cultural capital "is convertible, in certain conditions, into economic capital and may be institutionalized in the form of educational qualifications" (p. 16).	2b. **Economic capital** contributes to the development of **cultural capital** in the form of **educational qualifications** which, in turn, further contributes to **inequality.**
3a. **When** Amazon **bought** Whole Foods, **the employees** at Whole Foods didn't like **Jeff Bezos** so they started coming to work late, calling in sick, or simply quitting.	3b. The changes in **leadership** at Whole Foods contributed to employees' lack of **motivation and productivity.**

Without explicit instruction, some students struggle with writing paragraphs that start with a clear point or claim that uses abstractions to make a characterization or evaluation that is then defended in the paragraph. Instead, as shown in Table 3.2, students may start their paragraphs with an example (1a), a disciplinary definition (2a), or a narrative that focuses on concrete information with details from a case (3a).

These go against expectations for academic paragraphs that typically move from abstract to concrete or from decontextualized to contextualized. An example or a narrative (see examples 1a and 3a) immediately provides contextualized information, and the reader may find it difficult to understand its importance to the argument without being guided first with a claim. Readers of academic texts expect writers to start with a generalized point, a conclusion the writer has drawn, then support it with concrete and contextualized information. Fronting the general claim and then unpacking it in more specific ways in the paragraph aids the reader in processing information (Mitchell et al., 2021). Furthermore, a disciplinary definition (see example 2a) is a community-agreed-upon statement that does not need to be defended with reasons and evidence. In an argument, the reader wants to hear the writer's voice and wants the paragraph to be driven by the writer's position. Starting a paragraph with "According to Bourdieu, cultural capital is . . . " prevents the voice of the writer from driving the argument and/or paragraph.

With explicit instruction, students can write effective claims like 1b, 2b, and 3b in Table 3.2 that:

- use **disciplinary key words to package information**: *economic capital, cultural capital, formal and informal knowledge, leadership, motivation*;
- make a **characterization or evaluation**: *Students with **limited** economic capital **lack** formal or informal knowledge*; and
- **connect disciplinary key words using linking relations** (such as *be*) or **causal relations** (causes, results from, leads to, create, etc.): *The changes in leadership at Whole Foods **contributed to** employees' lack of motivation and productivity*.

3. What Resources Can We Use to Address the Problem?

3.1. What Is a Claim?

Following from the Onion Model, writing argumentatively involves making an explicit evaluation that typically unfolds with a claim that is supported with reasons and evidence. Thus, it is important to emphasize to students that a claim is an evaluative statement that needs to be defended. We need to be explicit about what a claim is and is not, as shown in Table 3.3.

Table 3.3: What Is a Claim?

Claims are <u>not</u> disciplinary definitions that a discourse community agrees upon.

Cultural capital is . . .
Social capital is . . .

Claims are <u>not</u> facts or uncontroversial representations of disciplinary knowledge:

Bourdieu describes three forms of capital.
A SWOT analysis identifies potential risks of investments.

Claims are <u>not</u> contextualized narratives that focus on characters, actions, and details:

*When Amazon **bought** Whole Foods, **the employees** at Whole Foods didn't like **Jeff Bezos** so they started coming to work late, calling in sick, or simply quitting.*

Claims are <u>statements that make an evaluation or characterization that needs to be defended with evidence</u> to answer questions such as *How? Why?*

*Access to quality education **is rare** for students who grow up with limited economic capital.*
Questions:
1. Why is access to quality education rare for students who grow up with limited economic capital?

Economic capital contributes to the development of cultural capital in the form of educational qualifications which, in turn, further contributes to inequality.
Questions:
1. How does economic capital contribute to the development of cultural capital?
2. How and why does cultural capital contribute to inequality?

Claims are statements that <u>pack information using disciplinary key words</u>.

***Upward mobility** through **education** is rare for students who grow up with limited **economic capital**.*

*For poor students, developing **cultural capital** through **education** can lead to **upward mobility**.*

The disciplinary words are often connected using:
• relational verbs (*to be, have*) and an adjective (e.g., *important, significant, limited*) to make an evaluation or a characterization
*Access to quality education **is rare** for students who grow up with limited economic capital.*
• causal relations with phrases or verbs such as *because, so, lead to, contribute to, affect, impact, create, cause* to show logical reasoning
*For poor students, developing cultural capital through education can **contribute** to upward mobility.*

From this explanation, it becomes apparent that disciplinary key words are an important resource to be able to write effective claims.

3.2. Using Disciplinary Key Words to Write Claims

Disciplinary key words are often abstract nouns or nominalizations, which SFL categorizes as *grammatical metaphors*: a phenomenon of *transcategorization*, whereby verbs, adjectives, or whole sentences are encoded as nouns. In the examples in Table 3.2, the more concrete phrasing of Whole Foods employees "*coming to work late, calling in sick, or simply quitting,*" realized in a series of verbs, is packaged into a more condensed, abstract form through the use of nominalizations (*employees' lack of motivation and productivity*). The effective use of grammatical metaphor has been associated with advanced complex writing demands such as the writing of logical arguments and persuasive evaluation (Ryshina-Pankova, 2010, 2015).

For writers of arguments, using abstractions helps make observations and generalizations beyond one specific exemplar. For example, when writing a Case Analysis based on Whole Foods, the writer can use abstractions such as *motivation* and *productivity* to extrapolate from the concrete and contextualized case of Whole Foods to more generalizable knowledge about organizational behavior.

These disciplinary key words or nominalizations are drawn from disciplinary frameworks or from phenomena each discipline is interested in. Let us examine the examples in Table 3.4.

Table 3.4: Examples of Claims Using Disciplinary Key Words

Organizational behavior	The adoption of the new **leadership style** poses a serious threat towards the **motivation** of the workface at Whole Foods.
Information systems	LEGO was successful in its implementation of **complementary innovation** as seen in LEGO's increase in sales and profit.
History	An analysis of Hammurabi's Code reveals great **gender inequality** as women had fewer rights in important matters such as divorce and marriage.
Sociology	**Immigration** economically and **culturally** enriches receiving countries.
Business	The **SWOT analysis** reveals that **investing** in solar energy in Qatar will generate high **revenue**.
Linguistics	**Standard language ideology** is problematic because it stigmatizes varieties used by poor and less educated people.

In the examples in Table 3.4, *leadership style* and *motivation* are disciplinary frameworks in the field of organizational behavior. As a framework, leadership style includes different types of leadership: telling, selling, participating, and delegating; motivation includes different types of motivation: intrinsic, extrinsic, etc. *Complementary innovation* is an element of the disciplinary framework of innovation, along with others such as incremental, product, and disruptive. *Standard language ideology* is a key concept in linguistics that is used to package all the different ideas that we may associate with users of stigmatized varieties of a language (e.g., African Americans are less intelligent because of how they use language; immigrants are lazy because they do not learn the "proper" way of talking).

The example from history uses *gender inequality* as a key word that embodies a social phenomenon that historians are interested in. The concept of gender inequality may not come directly from a disciplinary framework, but it is something that interests historians in the same way that they may be interested in social structure, judicial fairness, the impact of diseases, and the environment. Sociologists are interested in social phenomena such as immigration and its economic and cultural impact on society, while businesspeople do SWOT analysis to identify the risks of investments.

Identifying the disciplinary key words that are relevant to our analysis and argument requires some analytical work. We will return to this in Section 3.4.

3.3. Using Language From the Prompt to Write Claims

The kinds of key words that students draw on to write their claims may be informed by the key words in the writing prompts they receive from their teachers. In the history example in Table 3.4, this claim was written in response to the following prompt: *What does Hammurabi's Code reveal about the status of men and women in Ancient Babylonia?* Hammurabi's Code is a primary source that consists of a list of laws where the wording "gender inequality" is not used, but as the prompt alluded to differences between men and women, the writer was able to analyze the laws related to men and women and pack all the differences in the law into the phrase "great gender inequality."

Similarly, in the same history course, another prompt asked the student: *According to Hammurabi's Code, what kind of social structure did Ancient Babylonia have?* Again, Hammurabi's Code does not characterize the social structure of the time, but, as a student of history, the writer analyzed all the laws related to social structure and then packed and characterized the social structure as "class based."

When reading secondary texts, the writer may be able to use some of the key words from the prompt that are also used in the source text. Let us examine the writing prompts and claims from a history course in Table 3.5.

Writing Effective Claims: Key Words, Evaluations, and Causal Relations   55

Table 3.5: Writing Prompts and Claims in a History Class

Prompt: How **compelling** do you find McNeill's <u>argument</u> about the <u>impact of disease on culture?</u>	**Claim:** I find McNeill's <u>argument</u> about the <u>impact of disease on culture</u> compelling as clearly seen in the impact on <u>religion</u> and <u>social class</u>.
Prompt: How **compelling** do you find McNeill's argument about the impact of disease on culture?	**Claim:** From reading McNeill, it becomes clear that diseases **strongly** influenced <u>culture</u> in two main aspects: <u>religions</u> and <u>social classes</u>.
Prompt: How **convincing** do you find McNeill's <u>argument</u> that <u>disease</u> in Southern China slowed down <u>immigration</u> from China's North?	**Claim:** I find McNeill's <u>argument</u> convincing because he provides a scientific explanation as to how <u>disease</u> is generated and what causes it, and then why it represents a major <u>obstruction</u> for <u>immigration</u> from Northern China to its south.

Effective argumentative responses to these prompts:

- used the language of the prompt to formulate an evaluative thesis or claim: *I find the argument convincing/compelling*
- picked up on the disciplinary key words used in the prompt: *impact of disease on culture*
- used key words from the texts that include social phenomena historians are interested in: *religions and social classes*

In addition to using key words, these claims are also evaluative:

> *I find McNeill's argument **convincing** because he provides a scientific explanation as to how disease is generated and what causes it, and then why it represents a **major obstruction** for immigration from Northern China to its south.*

These claims also used causal relations to join key words and make an evaluative statement:

> *From reading McNeill, it becomes clear that diseases definitely **influenced** culture strongly in two main aspects: religions and social classes.*

> *I find McNeill's argument about the impact of disease on culture compelling **as** clearly seen in the impact on religion and social class.*

3.4. Generating Disciplinary Key Words to Write Claims

Coming up with the relevant key words from the discipline for the analysis and the argument requires some work. As explained in Chapter 2, in our first-year writing class, students use the disciplinary framework of Bourdieu's capital and the course readings on inequality to analyze a case related to inequality. To help students understand the process of analysis, we show students the visualization shown in Chapter 2 (Figure 2.4 and Figure 2.5) that exemplifies this process. Referring students to the visualization, we ask students to brainstorm ideas about their case and then brainstorm key words from their disciplinary knowledge about inequality and capital that relate to their case. The students are then asked to sort through their case data and group the data in relation to the disciplinary key words. We exemplify this process with the sample case of the student protests in Chile due to the inequalities associated with the university entrance examination (PSU, or SATs for ease of reference). Table 3.6 shows the disciplinary key words and the key words from the case, which would then serve as the starting point to make claims. Table 3.7 shows examples of claims about the SATs in Chile.

Table 3.6: Analyzing the SATs in Chile Through Bourdieu's Capital

Economic capital	Cultural capital	Social capital	Social class reproduction
Only students with families with **high incomes** can afford going to **private schools** to be better prepared for the SATs.	Students who attended **private schools** and attended the SAT college preparation program are more likely to pass the test (Khan).		**Accessing higher education in Chile is almost impossible for students of poor backgrounds,** thus **poverty is likely to be reproduced** in Chile (Lareau, 2002).
To pass the SATs, most students enroll in an **after-school program to prepare for the tests.** These programs are pricey so only students with families with **high incomes** can afford paying them.	Parents with **high levels of education** are likely to have **more information about the test,** how and where to prepare for the test, as opposed to students with parents with lower levels of education		To get out of poverty, poor students need **access to quality education** which is not **happening in Chile.**
Thus, the test is an example of **democratic inequality** disguised as **meritocracy.**			

Writing Effective Claims: Key Words, Evaluations, and Causal Relations   57

Table 3.7: Sample Claims About the Inequalities Associated With the SATs in Chile

1. The privatization of the school system in Chile has created unequal access to education, which contributes to the reproduction of economic inequality in ways that are harmful to society.
2. The perception of the SATs in Chile as an equalizer actually obscures the fact that society actually promotes "democratic inequality" disguised as meritocracy (Khan, 2011).
3. Parents with limited economic mobility are often unable to provide their children with chances to gain cultural capital necessary to become upwardly mobile.
4. Equal access to quality education is vital to reversing worldwide trends of economic inequality, but clearly in Chile such access is not currently provided.

The sample claims in Table 3.7 use:

- **disciplinary key words to package information**: *privatization, access to education, reproduction of economic inequality, democratic inequality, meritocracy, economic mobility, cultural capital, upwardly mobile, access to equality education, economic inequality*
- **evaluations**: *unable, necessary, vital, not currently provided, equal/ unequal*
- **causal relations to connect ideas together**: *created, contributes to, obscures*

Using this same process, students in our classes were able to identify a case, brainstorm key words and associated disciplinary key words, and write effective claims about their cases. See Table 3.8 for examples of two student Problem Analysis assignments from the same class. See Table 3.9 for two more examples from another class that focused on urbanism and problems associated with urban development. The disciplinary key words are in bold, and the evaluations are in bold and italicized.

Table 3.8: Sample Claims From Students' Problem Analysis Assignments Related to Inequality

Case 1: The IGCSE international British exam system	**Claim:** The IGCSE International British exam system *is biased* towards those with more **cultural capital** relevant to the exams, which is often developed in private schools that require a substantial amount of **economic capital** to attend.
	Supporting Claims: 1. The British examinations are *disguised as* **meritocracy** when in fact test results are correlated with students and parents' **economic and cultural capital.**

(Continued)

58 ANALYSIS AND ARGUMENT IN FIRST-YEAR WRITING AND BEYOND

Table 3.8: (Cont.)

	2. Even the re-grading system is *problematic* as it has a fee attached to it, so students with higher **economic capital** have more opportunity to score higher than others. 3. **The COVID-19 pandemic** made the **inequalities** associated with the test *greater* when students were not able to take the tests and results were based on the **socio-economic backgrounds** of a school's previous students.
Case 2: Elite universities in Vietnam	**Claim:** Unequal **access to universities** in Vietnam is *prevalent*, contributing to the **socio-economic gap** and **social class reproduction**. **Supporting Claims:** 1. Without a high level of **economic capital**, it is **difficult** for lower-income students to get admitted to Vietnamese elite universities. 2. The admission process in Vietnamese elite institutions is *disguised* as a **meritocracy**, while in fact, **cultural capital** transmitted from parents to children plays an important role in filtering candidates. 3. With guidance from parents, students from elite backgrounds have *more opportunities* to develop **social capital**, which is necessary for admission to and successful performance at university. 4. Ultimately, **social class reproduction** will be reinforced since the college environment provides resources for elite students to thrive in both an academic setting and the future workforce.

Table 3.9: Sample Claims From Students' Problem Analysis Assignments Related to Urbanization

Case 1: The Pearl in Qatar, a residential luxurious man-made island	**Claim:** In Qatar, **new urbanism developments** such as the Pearl have given the country an image of **modernization** and **globalization**; however, the Pearl has **failed to integrate** into the city and *has not lived up to* the **promises of new urbanism**. **Supporting Claims:** 1. The Pearl seems to have been built mostly for **symbolic power** and not to benefit all inhabitants. 2. It has contributed to **social segregation** as only a small sector of the population can afford living there. 3. It has also contributed to the **commercialization of public spaces** as it's full of high-end stores and cafes.
Case 2: Gawalmandi Food Street in Lahore, Pakistan	**Claim:** Gawalmandi Food Street in Lahore, Pakistan is *at risk* of losing its **authenticity** because **economic development** took precedence over **cultural preservation**. **Supporting Claims:** 1. With its local food stalls, smells, and sounds, Gawalmandi Food Street has breathed Lahore's **authenticity** for decades. 2. This **authenticity** may be *at risk* due to new urban developments that may contribute to **cultural erosion** and **gentrification**. 3. Despite all odds, the still *vibrant* scene at Gawalmandi Food Street shows promise that **cultural preservation** and **economic development** can co-exist is done properly.

3.5. From Isolated Claims to a Main Claim With Supporting Claims

While writing effective claims is an important step toward writing analytically and argumentatively, writers also need to have a clear understanding of what it is they want to argue and how they will support it to effectively come up with a main claim and supporting claims.

The main claim, or thesis, is the core answer to the question that is asked in the assignment or prompt. The thesis is developed by connecting a series of supporting claims to build the argument. Each supporting claim is supported with appropriate evidence.

Coming up with a main argument and supporting claims is content-specific as it depends on what you are writing about. Thus, this chapter cannot offer comprehensive strategies for writing claims in all classroom contexts. However, here are some tips that can help students write a main argument and supporting claims.

1. A main claim is the core answer to the question of the assignment or the prompt:

    Prompt: For your problem analysis, you will select a case related to privilege, and you will analyze it through Bourdieu's capital and what we have learned about inequality this semester. A case could be the story of a person you know, a group of people, or a community, a current event, or a social phenomenon that points to a problem related to inequality. You will use your analysis of your case to argue about the complexities and characteristics of the problem(s) associated with the case or what the case represents. To support your position, you will draw on details of the case and the course readings.

    Main claim: Unequal access to universities in Vietnam is prevalent, contributing to the socio-economic gap and social class reproduction.

2. The supporting claims are the reasons offered to support the main claim:

    a. *Without a high level of economic capital, it is difficult for lower-income students to get admitted to Vietnamese elite universities.*

    b. *The admission process in Vietnamese elite institutions is disguised as a meritocracy, while in fact, cultural capital transmitted from parents to children plays an important role in filtering candidates.*

ANALYSIS AND ARGUMENT IN FIRST-YEAR WRITING AND BEYOND

    c. *With guidance from parents, students from elite backgrounds have more opportunities to develop social capital, which is necessary for admission to and successful performance at university.*

    d. *Ultimately, social class reproduction will be reinforced since the college environment provides resources for elite students to thrive in both an academic setting and the future workforce.*

3. The reasons are packed into abstractions that are then developed into their own claims with appropriate evidence.

    a. *Without a high level of **economic capital**, it is **difficult** for lower-income students to get admitted to Vietnamese elite universities.*

    b. *The admission process in Vietnamese elite institutions is **disguised** as a **meritocracy**, while in fact, **cultural capital** transmitted from parents to children plays an important role in filtering candidates.*

    c. *With guidance from parents, students from elite backgrounds have **more opportunities** to develop **social capital**, which is necessary for admission to and successful performance at university.*

    d. *Ultimately, **social class reproduction** will be reinforced since the college environment provides resources for elite students to thrive in both an academic setting and the future workforce.*

4. The order of the supporting claims matters. Claims need to be presented in a logical order to effectively build the argument. Writers need to think about the hierarchy of their claims; which ones should go first, second, third, and why. Claim 1 leads to Claim 2 and together they lead to Claim 3. Without a logical sequence of claims, the text may turn into a list of isolated claims that do not contribute to a unified argument.

In the case of access to elite universities in Vietnam, the claims have an order that works for the logic of the argument. Supporting Claim 1 about economic capital comes first because it is elite parents' economic capital that determines the cultural and social capital of their children; these forms of capital will guarantee them access to and successful performance at these elite universities, which all together contribute to the process of social class reproduction. Starting with cultural or social capital would not make sense since it is economic capital that heavily influences the development of the other forms of capital.

Here is another example from a student Case Analysis about the banning of the hijab in France, from a first-year writing class on the topic of the common good.

Main Claim: *In discussions about the banning of the hijab in France, I argue that freedom of expression should be prioritized over state secularism . . .*
Supporting Claim 1: *. . . because the ban targets particular citizens and marginalizes them by creating divisions in society.*
Supporting Claim 2: *By targeting Muslims, the ban of the veil has been used for political reasons rather than its stated purpose of protecting neutrality.*
Supporting Claim 3: *Targeting Muslim minorities for political reasons puts at risk the role of statesmanship and institutions to counter divisions and to protect vulnerable minorities.*

In this example, each supporting claim leads to the other and builds on the key words used in the previous claim. This is a strategy that can help writers to order their claims effectively.

The lessons in this chapter will expand ways in which we can help students write effective claims that include disciplinary key words, evaluations, and causal relations.

4. Lessons

4.1. Which Claim Is More Effective?

In this lesson, you can provide students with the following pairs of claims, or you can come up with your own claims based on the content of your class. Following the guidelines discussed in this chapter, ask students to identify the most effective claim in each pair and explain their rationale.

Claim 1a: The man-made island The Pearl in Qatar was open in 2008 and it consists of various residential luxurious towers, townhouses, villas, shops, restaurants, that only some people can afford.
Claim 1b: The man-made island The Pearl in Qatar is a high-end new urbanism development which contributes to social segregation in Qatar.
Claim 2a: Hanok Village has lost the true soul of authentic Korean lifestyle and local identity because it feels almost like any other commercialized place except for its very traditional architecture.

Claim 2b: When I went to Seoul, I did a day trip to Hanok Village which is a traditional Korean village located on the top of a hill between three palaces.

Claim 3a: The adoption of the new leadership style poses as a serious threat towards *motivation* in the workforce.

Claim 3b: Motivation, according to Victor H. Vroom (as cited in Aworemi, Abdul-Azeez, & Durowojo, 2011) is prioritizing a choice among other "alternative forms of voluntary activities" (p. 78 Martinus, H., & Ramadanty, S., 2016), and the individual has complete autonomy over it.

Claim 4a: Many people enjoy that Zappos has a 24/7 work service. "Zappos is a web-based shoe store that became a billion-dollar company in ten years by focusing on delighting the customer."

Claim 4b: Zappos' 24/7 work service is highly valued by customers.

Claim 5a: The ancient Babylonia was divided into three classes: free people from the upper class, free people from law state, and slaves.

Claim 5b: The Babylonian social structure was essentially ruled by the class system, which can be seen by the difference in punishments by the law for committing a crime.

4.2. Identifying the Components of Effective Claims

You may use the claims in 4.1, the claims listed below, or claims of your own based on the content of your class and ask students to identify what makes the claims effective. The students may identify the use of the following linguistic resources in the claims to explain their <u>effectiveness</u>:

- use of disciplinary key words
- use of evaluative resources
- categorization or labeling of an issue
- causal relations

Claim 1: Despite the implementation of capital punishment in Pakistan, crime is still rampant and increasing day by day.

Claim 2: Capital punishment should not exist as a form of punishment because it is used against the poor people and minority groups.

Claim 3: The right to bear arms in the U.S. should be abolished because it is outdated and irrelevant to today's society.

Writing Effective Claims: Key Words, Evaluations, and Causal Relations 63

Claim 4: The right to bear arms has been politicalized and commercialized, purposes that have nothing to do with the original right to bear arms from the U.S. constitution.

Claim 5: The banning of the hijab in France is racist because it targets Muslims and marginalizes them by creating divisions in society.

4.3. Analyzing Cases, Generating Key Words, and Writing Claims

As mentioned in this chapter, in our first-year writing course, we have students write a Problem Analysis based on a case related to inequality chosen by each student. To scaffold this assignment, the process of analysis, and the writing of claims, we expose students to different cases early in the semester and have them analyze the cases using what they learned in class about inequality from the point of view of Bourdieu's capital.

Given the topic of your course, you can provide students with different cases and assign one case to a group of two to three students for analysis.

Our assignment guidelines ask students to do the following:

1. Make a list of key words that represent what we have learned about inequality this semester.
2. Familiarize yourselves with the case assigned to your group by reviewing the case material provided for each case: news articles, videos, and websites.
3. Using the questions provided by your professor, think about how the case relates to the course topic, readings, and discussion.
4. Make a list of key words that describe the case.
5. Underline the key words in your list that relate to our course readings and discussion.
6. Use the key words generated to make two to three claims about the case, using what we learned about writing effective claims.
7. Make a list of ideas that you can use to support your claims.

In our first-year writing course about inequality and privilege, we have asked students to analyze cases such as the following:

- the website of a given elite boarding school in Asia, Europe, or the U.S.
- a news article, documentary, or film about a current event related to educational inequalities or privilege, such as the 2018 college

admission scandal in the U.S. involving various celebrities or the 2020 postcode test scandal in the UK

- a news article, documentary, or film about a marginalized or oppressed group in a given region, such as the Uyghur Muslims in China

4.4. Revising Claims

Students do not always write claims that meet the expectations discussed in this chapter on their first try. An activity that can be done in class is to ask students to write their claims as part of their writing process, go over the students' claims in class, and provide feedback to revise them. In this lesson, we provide an original claim followed by its revised version. You can ask students to identify the changes that made the revised claim more effective. Alternatively, you can collect students' claims from their drafts, bring them to class, and have students revise them in pairs or in groups.

Original Claim 1: Those who go to Aitchinson College in Pakistan are rich students whose grandparents and parents were rich and whose children will be rich. My uncle Bilal went to Aitchinson and his grandparents and parents went to Aitchison College and his children are now going to Aitchinson.

Revised Claim 1: Elite educational institutions like Aitchison College contribute to the social class reproduction in Pakistan.

Original Claim 2: Operation Varsity Blues is a documentary that shows that people with money and connections such as actress Felicity Huffman can get their children into Harvard or Stanford even if their children don't have the credentials to be admitted.

Revised Claim 2: The recent college admissions scandal in the U.S. shows how high economic and social capital contributes to admission to prestigious universities.

Original Claim 3: Hammurabi's Code is a set of 232 laws from Ancient Babylonia that includes laws about how to run a state, how to punish people who commit crimes, and how to regulate commercial activities.

Revised Claim 3: Hammurabi's Code shows how people received different benefits and punishments based on their social class.

Original Claim 4: Some laws in Hammurabi's Code protected women as, for example, law 53 indicated that if a woman lost her husband, the state would help her support her children, but other laws favored men over women and gave women almost no rights.

Revised Claim 4: Although a few laws from Hammurabi's Code protected women, for the most part the laws showed great gender inequality in Babylonia.

Original Claim 5: My friends and I went to Al Hazam Mall last weekend, and we almost left the place immediately as we felt out place as we were the only non-Qatari people there and we felt very self-conscious to sit down at a café and not be able to afford almost anything on the menu as a coffee was about 15 dollars.

Revised Claim 5: Luxurious shopping malls like Al Hazam Mall in Doha, Qatar contributes to social segregation as they only cater to high-end consumers.

5. Concluding Remarks

In this chapter, we provided suggestions on how to help students write effective claims that use disciplinary key words and make an evaluation or characterization that needs to be defended with evidence. We have also provided suggestions for activities that can help students identify the components of effective claims, generate key words, and revise claims.

References

Coffin, C. (2006). *Historical discourse: The language of time, cause and evaluation*. Continuum.

Coffin, C., & Donohue, J. (2014). "This is description, not film analysis": Semiotically mediating genre, conceptual formations, and text development. *Language Learning, 64*, 85–145.

Dreyfus, S., Humphrey, S., Mahboob, A., & Martin, J. M. (2016). *Genre pedagogy in higher education. The SLATE project*. Palgrave Macmillan.

Duke, N. K., & Pearson, P. D. (2009). Effective practices for developing reading comprehension. *Journal of Education, 189*, 107–122.

Humphrey, S. (2013). And the word became text: A 4x4 toolkit for scaffolding writing in secondary English. *English in Australia, 48*, 46–55.

Humphrey, S., Sharpe, T. & Cullen, T. (2015). Peeling the PEEL: Integrating language and literacy in the middle years. *Literacy Learning: The Middle Years, 23*, 53–62.

Macnaught, L., Maton, K., Martin, J. R., & Matruglio, E. (2013). Jointly constructing semantic waves: Implications for teacher training. *Linguistics & Education*, *24*, 50–63.

Mitchell, T. D., Pessoa, S., Gómez-Laich, M. P., & Maune, M. (2021). Degrees of reasoning: Student uptake of a language-focused approach to scaffolding patterns of logical reasoning in the case analysis genre. *TESOL Quarterly, 55,* 1278–1310.

Ryshina-Pankova, M. (2010). Toward mastering the discourses of reasoning: Use of grammatical metaphor at advanced levels of foreign language acquisition. *The Modern Language Journal*, *94*, 181–197.

Ryshina-Pankova, M. (2015). A meaning-based approach to the study of complexity in L2 writing: The case of grammatical metaphor. *Journal of Second Language Writing 29*, 51–63.

Wingate, U. (2012). 'Argument!' helping students understand what essay writing is about. *Journal of English for Academic Purposes*, *11*, 145–154.

CHAPTER 4

I Know, I See, I Conclude: Resources to Help Students Adopt Effective Patterns of Analytical Writing

1. What Is the Expectation and What Is the Challenge for Students?

Even when students know how to distinguish between analysis and description (see Chapter 2) and how to write argumentative claims (see Chapter 3), they face challenges analyzing within argumentative paragraphs. That is, they struggle with weaving (abstract) disciplinary knowledge with (concrete) "data" (i.e., evidence or case information) to make conclusions. Doing so is a key aspect of analytical writing, yet students often do not know *how* to weave abstract and concrete information in support of their conclusions, or how to create logical connections between these different elements of their analytical paragraphs. They often rely heavily on logical relations of *addition*, where ones of *cause*, *consequence*, or *comparison* would better help them achieve their purpose. Even if students understand that they are supposed to do more than just re-present information from the case or display their understanding of disciplinary knowledge, they are challenged by how to do so.

This chapter focuses on how to help students use resources of logical reasoning to represent their analysis in writing effectively.

2. What Does the Challenge Look Like in First-Year Writing and in Writing in the Disciplines?

In the final paper for our first-year writing class, students write a paper where they make an original argument that contributes to the academic conversation we have read all semester. For this assignment, we expect students to develop supporting claims and evidence to bolster their main claim: they must draw on concepts from a course reading, apply an author's analysis of a particular case to their own case, or show how an author's claim reinforces their own observations about their case. Yet students are challenged by weaving these authoritative voices with both their own voice and the concrete details of their case. Even when students write argumentatively and connect their ideas logically, they sometimes struggle to connect disciplinary knowledge with "data."

The examples in Table 4.1 show contrasting student texts where writers struggled to connect disciplinary knowledge with data differently.

Table 4.1: Contrasting Texts Where Students Struggled to Connect Disciplinary Knowledge With Data

Text 1
It is very hard to create a project such as a mall, or a downtown that attracts both the higher and lower class. Qatar has a targeted audience wanting to make it a luxurious country. This does not mean that it tries to ignore the people living with lower economic conditions. For example, if you look at the pearl cinema which costs about 40 riyals per ticket not including popcorn and snacks. Or on the other hand gulf cinema costs about 10 riyals per ticket also not including popcorn and snacks therefore it's not that Qatar- designs its urban planning to discriminate against the lower class. They would rather go somewhere that can fit their budget. They are multiple of projects and malls in Qatar that target the lower class. Also, lots of public spaces that are filled on Fridays with the lower-class labor workers such as parks and public sports fields. Even looking at the future projects Mushairbs new downtown's main goal is "To promote social inclusion through the provision of housing for different social groups and classes and a mixture of single and family accommodation:" (Rania F. Khalil). There are lots of malls and future projects that focus on the lower class. Sadly, in this day and age you will find it difficult to see people from the lower class interact with people in the higher class that much. Not only in Qatar but around the world. You might see some minimal interaction, but it will not cause friendships.
Text 2
Due to social media, people have more friends and acquaintances outside then neighborhood, reducing the need for sidewalks as an integration medium. This is something Jane Jacobs could not have anticipated in 1966. Michael Crang (2007) illustrates this when he writes about how "communities consist of far-flung kinship, workplace, interest group, and neighborhood ties concatenating to form a network that provides aid, support, social

I Know, I See, I Conclude

Table 4.1: (Cont.)

control, and links to other milieus" (p. 2412). Furthermore, through this he is showing the complexity that occurs with real-life communities. Therefore, reinforcing the fact that social media makes connecting with people easier, since through social media you can get the benefits of density without having to be in close proximity to others, contradicting Glaeser's (2011) claim that "Cities need roads and buildings that enable people to live well and to connect easily with one another" (p. 13). A common response against my claim could be that excessive communication through the internet is unhealthy, and that face-to-face communication is essential. I frilly agree with that statement, believing that there needs to be a balance. However, we cannot overlook the advantages that social media brings. Research by Collin. Rahilly. Richardson and Third states that "Email, instant messaging and social networking sites can address new barriers young people may face to forming and maintaining positive social relationships. These barriers can include lack of safe, accessible, and welcoming places to gather" (p. 16/17). This demonstrates how social media can help achieve what sidewalk enterprises have failed to accomplish, including providing women with a way to socialize without having to endure travelling through the sidewalk, which help emphasize its importance even more. In addition to this, sometimes social media is the only outlet that certain members of the community feel that they have in order to feel like they belong there, "for some young people, particularly those who are marginalized, or otherwise socially isolated, online relationships provided a significant, and sometimes the only, opportunity for such socialization" (p. 17).

Text 1 focuses exclusively on details about the case, neglecting to use any disciplinary knowledge in support, even though the writer does provide substantial reasoning in support of his claim. For example, the writer could have made inferences in support of their argument by drawing on the ideas of a course author who studied how interactions between rich and poor in public spaces in Chile did not lead to productive social capital for the poor residents.

In Text 2, the writer focuses exclusively on how the arguments of others support their overall claim. Despite the writer's relatively strong reasoning and integration of authorial voices, they neglect to include any concrete evidence. For example, they could have focused more on the claim about women and used statistics or an anecdote about male-dominated public spaces in the Middle East or their own experiences being more comfortable building relationships with friends online.

It is important to note that both texts start with an argumentative claim and use logical reasoning to support it. In other words, these texts are not pure description of the case or re-presentation of the disciplinary knowledge like the ones we analyzed in Chapter 2. However, they are both still missing an important element in analytical and argumentative writing. We will look at these examples more closely later in this chapter.

In contrast to these two examples, the text in Table 4.2 connects disciplinary knowledge with evidence. The writer uses ideas from a course reading about the connection between cultural identity and physical places to explain the concrete details about their case study, Hanok Village, as described in a news article that the student found on their own.

Table 4.2: Student Text That Successfully Integrates Authors in Support of a Claim with Evidence From a Case

Hanok Village has lost the true soul of authentic Korean lifestyle and local identity because it feels almost like any other commercialized place except for its very traditional architecture. The cultural identity of a place can transcend the physical level i.e., it is not only represented within the buildings but also through the atmosphere of the place, which is mostly embodied and created by the residents of the place. Kong (2008) best summarizes this as she states, "the "spirit" and identity of place, rooted in history and community life, ate eroded with commercialization" (p. 363). The erosion of the spirit by commercialization can be witnessed as economic businesses that do not represent Korean culture and traditions flourish, as Kim (2015) states that there are "many shops selling Chinese-made goods, including selfie sticks and plastic toys." He further reports that the number of households that call the village home has dropped by nearly 50% in the past five years. This is evidence of the slow change of identity caused by the merge with the hegemonic global identity, which consequently led to a population shift of the residents outwards. Kong describes a possible outcome, which has already occurred in Chinatown in Singapore, as she states that during the night, it has the "silence of a ghost town without a soul in sight" (p. 361). Because it is catered to the users, the residents left Chinatown, effectively taking its soul with them, turning a bustling street culture and vitality into a mere tourist attraction that "closes" at night. Essentially, since the locals who give Hanok its spirit and real insight to how life is like in their respective culture are no longer present, it slowly shifts the ambiance of the place where it becomes more inauthentic. In other words, it no longer had a unique "personality" in a sense as it started to replicate the hegemonic global "soul."

The writer then draws further on the course reading to extract more meaning from the evidence they have presented. This paragraph represents the type of analytical reasoning and argumentative support that we want from our students, but the majority need explicit instruction to achieve it.

Something similar happens when students are asked to write case analyses in information systems and business administration, or to write arguments in history. When writing a Case Analysis, the point of the analysis is to persuasively argue for a claim about why a company has problems so the client will accept recommendations to address them. In such a classroom context, students must connect the case information to concepts from the discipline because academic theories are more powerful than commonsense ideas in their ability to explain problems in the case. This can be especially challenging for students when the disciplinary terms have commonsense meanings (e.g., *leadership* is both a specialized organizational behavior term and an everyday term). In such cases, students must take extra care to keep their analysis grounded in the technical definitions of these terms and how they apply to the case.

3. How Can We Help Students With This Challenge?

3.1. The Know-See-Conclude Heuristic

We use the *I know*, *I see*, *I conclude* heuristic that we adapted and simplified from Hao's (2020) SFL-based work on patterns of reasoning in students' biology lab reports. With this heuristic, we help students understand how to connect abstract disciplinary knowledge and concrete information. Specifically, this tool helps students implement patterns of reasoning to integrate what they "know" from the discipline and its authoritative voices (e.g., Kong's claims about the relationship between commercialization and authenticity) with what they "see" in the case (e.g., the sale of Chinese goods in the traditional Korean village as evidence of inauthenticity), eventually leading to conclusions. The conclusions represent an understanding of the case/evidence through the lens of the disciplinary knowledge. By applying a disciplinary framework, theory, or relevant authoritative information to the details of the particular case, the student creates "new" knowledge, knowledge which may be more tentative ("I think") or certain ("I conclude"). Figure 4.1 summarizes how a student needs to move between *know* and *see* moves in support of a claim so that they arrive at a conclusion.

The know-see-conclude heuristic is not a formula, so it is important to emphasize to students that there are many possibilities for the logical development of information in analytical paragraphs. One way of showing them possibilities for variation is by providing explicit language resources that allow writers to effectively connect information within a paragraph.

Specifically, we can provide students with resources to show their reasoning by connecting the reasoning positions established in their *know*, *see*, and *conclude* moves. There are resources that organize arguments, such as *in conclusion* and *moreover* (Martin, 1992), and resources that establish logical relationships between claims and reasons, such the cause-and-effect relationships realized by conjunctions like *because*, *as*, *thus*, and *therefore*. The visualization in Figure 4.2 summarizes these resources and shows the corresponding icons we use to annotate sample texts.

Figure 4.1: Visualization of the I Know, I See, I Conclude Heuristic

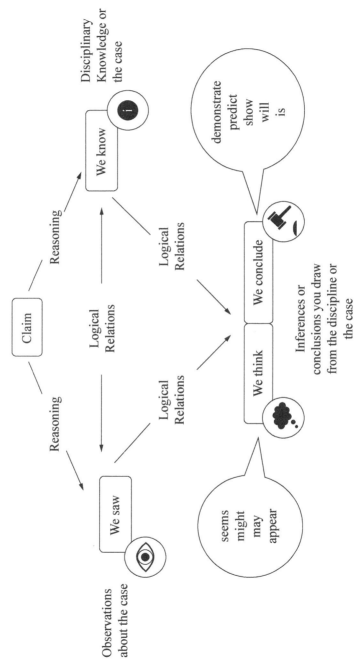

Connecting **what you saw** to **what you know** in order to show **what you think or conclude** is how you generate **new knowledge** within a discipline.

I Know, I See, I Conclude

Figure 4.2: A Taxonomy of Logical Relationships and Corresponding Language to Articulate Them

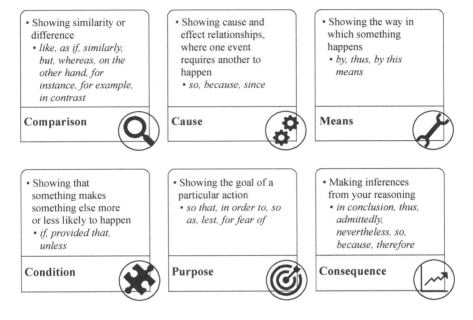

4. Lessons

4.1. Visualizing Information Flow to Avoid "Flatlines" of Meaning

We suggest creating visualizations of sample texts that segment *know, see,* and *conclude* moves and overlaying them with lines that indicate how information oscillates from more abstract to more concrete, creating waves of meaning (Maton, 2014). The knowledge presented in an analytical paragraph can range from very abstract—and therefore less dependent on context of the case—to more concrete—and therefore more dependent on context. Strong analytical writing represents meanings that move between abstract course concepts (e.g., *social capital, social class mobility, meritocracy*) and concrete evidence (e.g., *working class students in Santiago are 30% less likely to attend university*).

The first step is to help students understand that it is important to avoid meaning "flatlines" (Maton, 2014, p. 121), texts that focus exclusively on disciplinary knowledge or concrete evidence. In Table 4.3, we show the text that makes claims only about what the writer "sees" in the case of Qatar, but without any disciplinary concepts to inform their observations. In this text, the writer only articulates commonsense understandings of their home city. Even so, it is important to notice that the writer is using logical reasoning to support their position about urban planning in Qatar, particularly relations of comparison to provide examples and consequence to draw conclusions about them. Most of the building blocks of a strong paragraph are present, but the disciplinary-based analysis is missing. Although we present examples from our own students' work, we encourage instructors to create their own visualizations with their students' texts.

Table 4.3: Visualization of Sample Student Text With a Flatline of Meaning

Type of logical reasoning	I see	I know
	It is very hard to create a project such as a mall, or a downtown that attracts both the higher and lower class.	
Cause	Qatar has a targeted audience wanting to make it a luxurious country.	
Consequence	This does not mean that it tries to ignore the people living with lower economic conditions.	
Comparison	For example, if you look at the pearl cinema which costs about 40 riyals per ticket not including popcorn and snacks.	
Consequence	They would rather go somewhere that can fit their budget.	
Addition	There are multiple of projects and malls in Qatar that target the lower class	
Addition	Also, lots of public spaces that are filled on Fridays with the lower-class labor workers such as parks and public sports fields	
Comparison	Even looking at the future projects Mushairbs new downtown's main goal is "To promote social inclusion through the provision of housing for different social groups and classes and a mixture of single and family accommodation," (Rania F. Khalil).	

I Know, I See, I Conclude

Table 4.3: (Cont.)

Type of logical reasoning	I see	I know
Addition	There are lots of malls and future projects that focus on the lower class. Not only in Qatar but around the world.	
Consequence	You might see some minimal interaction, but it will not cause friendships.	

In Table 4.4, on the other hand, the writer does not make any references to a specific case, but instead reasons about the role of social media in creating social connections. The writer's larger argument was about how the public spaces of neighborhood streets in Qatar do not produce the same type of social interactions that were described by an author we read in the course, yet in this paragraph they do not mention Qatar or provide any specific details about local interactions. Even so, the writer does use logical relations of consequence and comparison to weave their perspective within the scholarly conversation, showing how certain authors support their position and allow the writer to reject potential disagreements.

Table 4.4: Visualization of Sample Student Text With a Flatline of Meaning

Type of logical reasoning	I see	I know
		Due to social media, people have more friends and acquaintances outside their neighborhood, reducing the need for sidewalks as an integration medium.
Consequence		This is something Jane Jacobs could not have anticipated in 1966.
Comparison		Michael Crang (2007) illustrates this when he writes about how "communities consist of far-flung kinship, workplace, interest group, and neighborhood ties concatenating to form a network that provides aid, support, social control, and links to other milieus" (p. 2412).
Addition		Furthermore, through this he is showing the complexity that occurs with real-life communities.
Consequence		Therefore, reinforcing the fact that social media makes connecting with people easier, since through social media you can get the benefits of density without having to be in close proximity to others,

(Continued)

76   ANALYSIS AND ARGUMENT IN FIRST-YEAR WRITING AND BEYOND

Table 4.4: (Cont.)

Type of logical reasoning	I see	I know
Comparison		contradicting Glaeser's (2011) claim that "Cities need roads and buildings that enable people to live well and to connect easily with one another" (p. 13).
Consequence		A common response against my claim could be that excessive communication through the internet is unhealthy, and that face-to-face communication is essential.
Addition		And I fully agree with that statement, believing that there needs to be balance.
Comparison		However, we cannot overlook the advantages that social media brings.
Means		Research by Collin, Rahilly, Richardson and Third states that "Email, instant messaging and social networking sites can address new barriers young people may face to forming and maintaining positive social relationships.
Means		These barriers can include lack of safe, accessible, and welcoming places to gather" (p. 16/17).
Consequence		This demonstrates how social media can help achieve what sidewalk enterprises have failed to accomplish, including providing women with a way to socialize without having to endure travelling through the sidewalk, which help emphasize its importance even more.
Addition		In addition to this, sometimes social media is the only outlet that certain members of the community feel that they have in order to feel like they belong there, "for some young people, particularly those who are marginalized, or otherwise socially isolated, online relationships provided a significant, and sometimes the only, opportunity for such socialization" (p. 17).

4.2. Visualizing Effective Waves of Meaning

You can contrast the texts from Section 4.1 with the texts in Table 4.5, where the writer uses the disciplinary knowledge to analyze the case, creating waves of meaning. Call students' attention to the movement from abstract, specialized terminology and references to scholarly support to the concrete details about the cultural village. It is important to explain how the *conclude* moves use the course concepts to inform the reader's understanding about the case information, creating new knowledge about it. In the *conclude* moves, the writer uses concepts like *authenticity*, *commercialization*, and *cultural identity* to analyze the Korean cultural village. *Conclude* moves are marked in bold and span both columns, which indicates the blending of disciplinary knowledge with case information. Once again, we encourage instructors to create their own visualizations with their students' texts.

Table 4.5: Visualization of Sample Student Text With an Effective Wave of Meaning

Type of logical reasoning	I see	I know
	(Claim) **Hanok Village has lost true soul of authentic Korean lifestyle and local identity because it feels almost like any other commercialized place except for its very traditional architecture.**	
Addition		The cultural identity of a place can transcend the physical level i.e., it is not only represented within the buildings but also through the atmosphere of the place, which is mostly embodied and created by the residents of the place. Kong (2008) best summarizes this as she states, "the "spirit" and identity of place, rooted in history and community life, are eroded with commercialization" (p. 363)
Consequence	**The erosion of the spirit by commercialization can be witnessed as economic business that do not represent Korean culture and traditions flourish**	
Comparison (for example)	as Kim (2015) states that there are "many shops selling Chinese-made goods, including selfie sticks and plastic toys." He further reports that the number of households that call the village home has dropped by nearly 50% in the past five years.	

(*Continued*)

78 ANALYSIS AND ARGUMENT IN FIRST-YEAR WRITING AND BEYOND

Table 4.5: (Cont.)

Type of logical reasoning	I see	I know
Consequence	This is evidence of the slow change of identity caused by the merge with the hegemonic global identity, which consequently led to a population shift of the residents outwards.	
Consequence		Kong describes a possible outcome, which has already occurred in Chinatown in Singapore, as she states that during the night, it has the "silence of a ghost town without a soul in sight" (p. 361)
Cause		Because it is catered to the users, the residents left Chinatown, effectively taking its soul with them, turning a bustling street culture and validity into a more tourist attraction that "closes" at night.
Consequence	Essentially, since the locals who give Hanok its spirit and real insight to how life is like in their respective culture are no longer present, it slowly shifts the ambiance of the place where it becomes more inauthentic. In other words, it no longer had a unique 'personality' in a sense as it stared to replicate the hegemonic global 'soul.'	

To reinforce the idea that this is a heuristic, not a template or formula, show the students another example of a text that effectively oscillates between abstract and concrete information, but with a different pattern of moves and different logical relations connecting them (see Table 4.6). Explain to students that relations of consequence are often useful for *conclude* moves and relations of comparison are often useful for *see* moves, but that these writers draw on other relations to make these moves and use these relations for other moves, too. Call students' attention to the variety of logical relations in each of these paragraphs and warn them against relying too heavily on relations of addition.

I Know, I See, I Conclude

Table 4.6: Visualization of Sample Student Text With an Effective Wave of Meaning

Type of logical reasoning	I see	I know
	(Claim) **The adoption of the new leadership style at Whole Foods poses a serious threat to employee empowerment by decreasing intrinsic *motivation*.**	
Addition		Motivation is strongly linked to job performance, but there are multiple ways motivation occurs (Konopaske et al., 2018).
Condition		When employees have intrinsic motivation, "outcomes [are achieved] from the application of individual ability and talent" (p. 135).
Addition	Before the acquisition of Whole Foods, employees were able to make their own choices in regards to selecting suppliers, judging product quality, and displaying products (HBS Working Knowledge, 2018).	
Consequence	**Thus, this leadership style provided a source of intrinsic motivation.**	
Comparison	After the acquisition, however, new policies were enforced to make operations cheaper and more efficient.	
Consequence	As a part of this change, a system called "order-to-shelf" was introduced, which sets strict logistical policies that essentially take away employees' autonomy.	
Addition	Additionally, evaluation tests described as "onerous, and stress-inducing" by employees were initiated;	
Consequence	failing these tests could result in being fired (Peterson, 2018).	
Consequence	**As a result of these changes, intrinsic motivation was largely replaced by extrinsic motivation,**	
Addition		which is motivation that is driven by external reward or a fear of consequences (Tranquillo & Stecker, 2016).
Addition		While extrinsic motivation may lead to initial increased productivity, intrinsic motivation has been shown to be more effective in the long-term (Tranquillo & Stecker, 2016).
Consequence	**Consequently, Amazon's different leadership style may have a negative effect on employee performance.**	

80   ANALYSIS AND ARGUMENT IN FIRST-YEAR WRITING AND BEYOND

4.3. Practice With Identifying Flatlines of Meaning

To reinforce what they learned from Section 4.1, ask students to identify sentences or clauses in a paragraph as either disciplinary knowledge, concrete evidence, or disciplinary knowledge applied to concrete evidence. The examples presented here do not oscillate much, if it all, so they are helpful in allowing students to see what to avoid in their own writing.

You can use the texts presented here or create your own that are relevant to your discipline and course topic. After students have attempted to identify the information, you can show them the visualization with the "wave." You can use these examples along with those in Section 4.4 or start the students with these and then move on to the more nuanced texts.

Table 4.7: Exercise for Students to Identify Flatlines of Meaning in Sample Paragraphs

---

Example 1:
In fact, the new analysis, provided by Johns Hopkins Center for Health Equity and included in the Urban League's report, shows that the coronavirus infection rate for Blacks is 62 per 10,000, compared with 23 per 10,000 for whites. For death rates, it's even worse, an article from the Guardian states that "African Americans have died at a rate of 50.3 per 100.000 people, compared with 20.7 for whites. 22.9 for Latinos and 22.7 for Asian Americans." (Ed Pilkington. 2020). Furthermore, a study conducted by Elizabeth Wrigley-Field. 2020shows that "For White mortality in 2020 to reach levels that Blacks experience outside of pandemics, current COVID-19 mortality levels would need to increase by a factor of nearly 6. Moreover. White life expectancy in 2020 will remain higher than Black life expectancy has ever been unless nearly 700,000 excess White deaths occur" (p. 1). A poll conducted by Washington Post-Ipsos finds that 20 percent of Hispanic adults and 16 percent of blacks report being laid off or furloughed since the outbreak began in the United States, compared with 11 percent of whites and 12 percent of workers of other races, this is explained hi the same article that states "Black and Hispanic workers are bearing the brunt of the economic crisis because they are overrepresented in industries that were hit first by social distancing mandates and stay-at-home orders, economists say.". The article also goes on to confirming that "the black unemployment rate, which is typically double that of whites, can be expected to reach nearly 30 percent". Clearly, black African Americans' lives have been more negatively affected by the pandemic than White Americans' lives in many ways.

I Know, I See, I Conclude

Table 4.7: (Cont.)

Case information	Disciplinary knowledge applied to case information	Disciplinary knowledge

Example 2:
Many people enjoy that Zappos has a 24/7 work service. "Zappos is a web-based shoe store that became a billion-dollar company in ten years by focusing on delighting the customer. Its CEO. Tony Hsieh, explains how this works: Zappos runs its warehouse 24/7 which isn't the most efficient way to run a warehouse, but it is the way in which Zappos can delight its customers. When a customer orders by midnight, and asks for (free) two-day shipping, he or she is pleasantly surprised when the order shows up on the doorstep eight hours later. Everything that happens hi Zappos is aimed at creating a "Wow!" experience for their customers" (Denning, 2011). Having a 24/7 service will mean that there are people working late hours or during the holidays. If no one is willing to work on holidays such as Christmas or other cultural holidays the company will be short of employees.

Case information	Disciplinary knowledge applied to case information	Disciplinary knowledge

4.4. Identify *Know, See,* and *Conclude* Moves

Now that the students know what to avoid, have them practice with paragraphs that oscillate between *know, see,* and *conclude* moves effectively. Ask the students to identify each move by filling in the blank table below (Table 4.8). For more advanced discussions, you can unpack the logical

82   ANALYSIS AND ARGUMENT IN FIRST-YEAR WRITING AND BEYOND

relationships that connect the moves. We have modeled this process with the first paragraph (Table 4.9) and its visualization (Figure 4.3). For the exercise, you can use the paragraphs in Tables 4.10 and 4.11 or provide your own.

Table 4.8: Exercise for Students to Identify Know, See, and Conclude Moves in Sample Paragraphs

I see in the case	I conclude about the case from my analysis using core concepts and authors	I know from course concepts and authors

Table 4.9: Model Paragraph for Unpacking the Logical Relationships that Connect the Know, See, and Conclude Moves

Not only has the leadership changed its priorities, it has also changed its leadership style which has negatively affected the culture of high achievement at MU. Leadership style, using Hersey-Blanchard's Situational Leadership Model (1988), depends primarily on three factors: follower readiness, relationship behavior, and task behavior. At MU, the leadership had developed a culture that made the faculty and staff "able and willing" to do their jobs and fulfill the university's mission. The faculty taught high quality classes as evident in student evaluations, secured competitive research funding, and published in high tier journals. This is indicative of the high follower readiness (Konopaske et al., 2018, p. 416). In such a situation, Hersey-Blanchard's model predicts an appropriate leadership style would have low task behavior, either leaving much of the direction of the faculty and staff to themselves or sharing in governance of the institution. In contrast, the new leadership at MU seems to have adopted a Telling leadership style. According to Konopaske et al. (2018), this leadership style results in high task behavior such as placing many demands on employees and low relationship behavior such as the employees not having time to develop interpersonal relationships. This style is evident in the required monthly performance reviews and the proliferation of new and detailed policies and procedures at every level of the organization. One faculty member commented that, "With the monthly performance reviews and all the paperwork that I need to do has created extra stress. I notice that my colleagues and I rarely have time for daily conversations that make coming to work more enjoyable" (Raji, 2020, p. 302). The mismatch between the high readiness of the employees and the high task behavior of the leadership has created a tension between management and labor while also doing damage to the culture of high achievement that had already been established.

I Know, I See, I Conclude

Figure 4.3: Visualization of the Model Paragraph Illustrating Know, See, and Conclude Moves and Types of Logical Reasoning

Position	Case Information	Organizational Behavior Knowledge
Claim (Preview)	The <u>leadership style</u> of the new management at MU seems to be a primary point of friction.	
I know		<u>Leadership style</u>, using Hersey-Blanchard's Situational Leadership Model (1988), depends on primarily three factors: <u>follower readiness</u>, <u>relationship behavior</u>, and <u>task behavior</u>.
I saw	**At MU**, the leadership had developed a culture that made the faculty and staff "able and willing" to do their jobs and fulfill the University's mission.	
I conclude	**demonstrating** that they had high <u>follower readiness</u> (Konopaske et al., 2018, p. 416).	
I know		**In such a situation**, Hersey-Blanchard's model **predicts** an appropriate <u>leadership style</u> would have <u>low task behavior</u>, either leaving much of the direction of the faculty and staff to themselves or sharing in governance of the institution.
I think	**In contrast**, the new <u>leadership</u> at MU **seems** to have adopted a <u>Telling Leadership style</u>, with <u>high task behavior</u> and <u>low</u> relationship behavior.	
I saw	This style **has been shown** in the institution of monthly performance reviews and the proliferation of new and detailed policies and procedures at every level of the organization.	
I conclude	The mismatch between the <u>high readiness</u> of the employees and the <u>high task behavior</u> of the leadership **has created** a tension between management and labor while also doing damage to the culture of high achievement that had already been established.	

Table 4.10: Sample Paragraph for Students to Identify Know, See, and Conclude Moves

Sample Paragraph 1:

The Chilean student protests are symptoms of inequality caused by the PSU being a "false equalizer." In other words, the exam gives the impression creating fairness, a beneficial tool of meritocracy, when in fact it is a problematic tool that reproduces economic inequality. Khan (2011) is highly critical of the idea of meritocracy, blaming it for the "democratic inequality" that makes society seem more open for more diverse groups even as it becomes more economically unequal: "[the] meritocracy of hard work and achievement has naturalized socially constituted distinctions, making differences in outcomes appear a product of who people are rather than a product of the conditions of their making" (p. 9). This exact idea applies to the case of the Chilean PSU, where only 30% of public-school students score high enough to qualify for college, compared to around 80% of private school students (Nugent, 2020). Only 6 out of 10 students' parents can afford to pay for private or semi-private schooling (Nugent, 2020). And of those who go to private schooling, 80% of them must pay for special classes after school to prepare for the PSU. Clearly, the current system is placing a significant portion of the Chilean population at disadvantage, greatly contributing to increasing inequality. The Latin American Inequality Index (2019) places Chile as the country with the highest level of inequality in Latin America. Such high levels of inequality have significant negative consequences for access to quality education and ensuring socio-economic mobility. If all students are not given an equal chance to be adequately prepared for the PSU, then students' performance on it does not reflect a true meritocracy. According to Khan (2011), meritocracy . . . . The economic inequality in Chile means that the exam scores are more a product of the conditions of students' making than of who they are. This type of educational system reproduces inequality across generations.

Table 4.11: Sample Paragraph for Students to Identify Know, See, and Conclude Moves

Sample Paragraph 2:

The underlying causes behind the higher number of affected African Americans seem to be rooted in systemic racism and the racial wealth gap, which contribute to discrimination in health services.

African Americans discrimination in health services is a consequence of the racial wealth gap that exists in the U.S, which is in turn a result of the persisting systemic racism in the U.S. Hannah-Jones (2020) talks about systemic racism and the consequences of the racial wealth gap saying "Wealth, not income, is the means to security in America . . . . It's not incidental that wealthier people are healthier and live longer" (p. 34). People who possess economic capital receive better health care and end up with a lower mortality rate. Clearly, discrimination has become embedded in the health care system. The inequalities in the health care system are quite evident in the case of poor African Americans during the covid-19 pandemic. In fact, the 2020 SOBA (State of Black America) report states that "Black people with COVID-19 symptoms in February and March were less likely to get tested or treated than white patients". In the same report, "Studies showed that doctors downplayed Black patients' complaints of pain, prescribed weaker pain medication and withheld car

Table 4.11: (Cont.)

> diac treatments from Black patients who needed them. Eligon and Burch (2020) suggest in *The New York Times* that the decisions are the result of "ingrained assumptions, cultural ignorance and hostile attitudes toward African-Americans" This emphasizes the impact of racial injustice and systemic racism on health care quality. Ehrenreich also explains the challenges of the poor stating "If you have no money for health insurance, you go without routine care or prescription drugs and end up paying the price" (p. 110), in this case black African Americans are paying the price with their lives. The 2020 SOBA report also states that Blacks and Latinos are less likely than whites to have health insurance, hence are less likely to rush for health care in hospitals. Poor African Americans' lack of health insurance is again a result of the racial wealth gap that exists in the U.S, which is in turn a result of the engrained systemic racism in the U.S. Systemic racism as well as the racial wealth gap introduce discrimination and inequality to health services against Black Americans.

5. Concluding Remarks

The language-focused tools presented can be applied to genres in many contexts requiring analytical and argumentative writing. Instructors can examine genres they teach to uncover valued ways of reasoning and building knowledge. We have found that explicitly articulating *what it means to analyze*—teaching students to see disciplinary knowledge as comprising frameworks to be applied to "data"—is a powerful beginning step. Then, supplementing their understanding of analysis with explicit resources for *how to represent analysis in writing*—such as the wave and know-see-conclude heuristics—is a valuable way of equipping students with tools that demystify complex processes.

References

Hao, J. (2020). *Analysing scientific discourse from a systemic functional linguistic perspective: A framework for exploring knowledge-building in biology*. Routledge.

Martin, J. R. (1992). *English text: System and structure*. John Benjamins.

Maton, K. (2014). *Knowledge and Knowers: Towards a realist sociology of education*. Routledge.

CHAPTER 5

Engagement: Resources to Help Students Align the Reader Toward the Writer's Perspective

1. What Is the Expectation and What Is the Challenge for Students?

Students are expected to write argumentative paragraphs that advance their overall claim. To do this, students need to integrate authoritative voices in support of their argument while maintaining a consistent position and aligning the reader to it. They need to anticipate the reader's expectations and make careful choices about how to manage them using interpersonal resources.

However, students experience difficulties using interpersonal resources to strategically manage multiple perspectives. Sometimes they neglect to include outside voices or articulate how source-based evidence relates to their claims. Other times, they position the reader inconsistently, which weakens the argument or makes the student's argumentative position less clear.

This chapter focuses on how to help students use interpersonal resources to align the reader to their perspective.

2. What Does the Challenge Look Like in First-Year Writing and in Writing in the Disciplines?

Sometimes students do not understand the persuasive goal of the arguments they are asked to write, so they respond with texts that re-present

Engagement

information from the sources they have read as if it were factual, rather using the sources to support an argument.

In our first-year writing courses, we have assigned students to write an analysis of an academic argument that requires them to identify the author's main claim and supporting claims, and to write an argument about how the author supports these claims with evidence; this means that students have to keep the author in focus while also making their own claims about how the evidence from different parts of the source text works together to support the author's overall argument. Sometimes students are challenged by this aspect of the task; they might mention the source text author at the start of the paragraph but then move to summarizing the text without attributing the ideas to the author and commenting on how they work to support the author's claim.

Text 1 illustrates this challenge. The writer begins with a claim about the author's argument but presents the rest of the information in the paragraph as if it were factual rather than as part of an argument that the author supports with evidence; the writer does not attribute the information to the author or provide quotations from the text to support the presented interpretation. Thus, the writer is challenged by how to weave their own voice with that of the source text author.

TEXT 1

Zukin argues that authenticity in a city is found in social diversity. This happens when new residents move in without making things too expensive for the longtime residents who give the place its character. Too often policy makers equate authenticity with preservation of historic buildings while ignoring the human element. They ignore the longtime residents, and everything gets replaced by what is trendy and new. Policies that maintain social diversity create situations where people of high income shop in international brands stores in the same neighborhood where middle- and low-income residents choose to shop in a mom-and-pop business. Neighbors are of different ethnicities, demand in stores is diversified, two different qualities of buildings exist opposite side of each other, and a public park has kids of different social classes playing together.

This challenge can be even more pronounced in history courses, where university history instructors usually assign argumentative writing, but students are accustomed to reading textbooks that present historical information as factual. When writing arguments in history courses, instructors expect students to engage with the contingent nature of historical texts. This means that students need to consider how all accounts of the past are written from a particular perspective.

Text 2 is a body paragraph from a history argument where the student was asked to read some of the laws from Hammurabi's Code and respond to the following prompt: *What sort of picture do you get about the treatment of women in ancient Babylonia?* In this response, the writer overwhelmingly uses the simple past tense; the writer does not use language resources to suggest other possible interpretations of the sequence of events or bring direct evidence from the source text. Thus, the writer does not demonstrate an awareness of the need to persuade the reader of an interpretation of historical evidence.

TEXT 2

The treatment of women in ancient Babylon was unfair. The laws created different punishments for men and women. Women received punishments for actions that were permissible for the men. The wife received benefits when there were children involved. The laws disregarded the women who had no children.

In other cases, students demonstrate an understanding of the need to bring in authoritative voices from sources but do not integrate these voices into their arguments effectively. Rather than seeing the evidence from the source text as something that needs to be explicitly linked to the overall argument so that the reader understands its role, some students just insert quotations with no attribution or explanation, as if the textual evidence speaks for itself, or they end the paragraph with a quotation without unpacking its significance and how it contributes to the points being developed.

Text 3, a body paragraph from the same assignment as Text 2, illustrates these two challenges with integrating source texts. Instead of making explicit the source of the quotation and explaining how this evidence furthers the claim about beneficial rules, the writer ends the paragraph with an unattributed quotation that leaves the reader to interpret its meaning.

Engagement

TEXT 3

Besides these cruel conditions for women, there were a few beneficial rules for the women. Babylonian society actually provided some rights for women. The women had the privilege to own their husband's property legally if their husband left them and their children. Women could get a part of their husband's assets to live their rest of the lives. "If a man wishes to separate from a woman who has borne him children, or from his wife who has borne him children: then he shall give that wife her dowry, and a part of the usufruct of field, garden, and property, so that she can rear her children."

Sometimes students do use resources that are meant to move the reader toward their position, but they are challenged by how to do so consistently. Strong argument usually requires students to consider and refute potential counterarguments, but this involves careful choices that can be difficult to manage.

Text 4 is a paragraph from an argument from a history class written in response to the following prompt: *To what extent was the women's movement successful in Europe in the early 20th century?* In Text 4, there are so many uses of *although* and *however* that it is difficult for the reader to interpret the writer's position on the information being presented. The paragraph is not focused on a clear claim, so the reader is seemingly positioned as someone who might think suffrage was a top-down process, someone who might think it was a bottom-up movement, someone who might not realize it was successful, and someone who might think it was a fast process throughout Europe. Thus, the writer demonstrates an awareness of the need to move the reader away from potential misconceptions but does not clearly guide the reader toward a clear overall, coherent claim.

TEXT 4

One of the greatest achievements of the woman emancipation movement in Europe was their access to voting rights. In her book, Sylvia Paletschek claims that "in most countries, this goal was achieved quickly, within the first two decades of the twentieth century," and explains that "the First world War was a turning point for the majority of European women's emancipation movements" (3). She further adds that this was aided by the fact that women were able to emphasize on the role they played during the war and the many reforms in political systems that followed its end. Women at that time considered this as a step towards modernity and utilized the social, democratic, and liberal parties to help achieve their goal. **Although** feminist leaders temporarily paused their campaigns during the years of the war, they continued to hope that the government would recognize their services in the war and grant them the right to vote. **Although** there are those who claim that women's access to suffrage in Europe was a top-down process from the government, in his article, Rubio-Marín explains that **although** there were many underlying factors (including the church and confessional parties), it was due to the effort women put in firm, organized labor of feminist suffrage movements that explain why some countries were quicker than others in granting women the right to vote (19). **However,** it is still believed that in some countries, it was in fact a top-down process as women suffrage had become "international standards, world culture and isomorphism" and countries felt obliged to comply with modern democratic systems (Ramirez, Soysal, and Shanaha). Therefore, it can be argued the suffrage movement was successful in the sense that it was a chain reaction whereby the success of one organization catalyzed the rest of the movement. **However,** that is not to say that most suffrage movements in Europe were as fast. In France, women were not allowed access to suffrage until the end of another war in 1944, and in Switzerland, attempts by The Swiss Association for Women Suffrage to gain the right to vote in 1918 for women were not successful.

We can contrast the previous examples with Text 5, a paragraph from a different argument written in response to the same prompt as Text 4. In Text 5, the student incorporates outside voices effectively to support the claim and moves the reader toward a clearly articulated position while anticipating alternative perspectives.

TEXT 5

Although women achieved suffrage, women's fight for citizenship was not as successful in Europe during the early 20th century. According to Ruiz and Rubio-Marín, "the political status of women cannot be fully understood without considering all aspects of citizenship" (136). This means that the right to vote did not guarantee full political participation for many women. For example, after women's suffrage began, in most European countries, women were only allowed to participate in political activities if they were citizens, and their only way to express their political opinions was through organizational work, journalism, and community activism. Furthermore, according to Ruiz and Rubio-Marín, German women automatically lost their citizenship if they married a foreigner until 1953, and these women were unable to pass citizenship to their children until the decision of the German Federal Constitutional Court in 1974 (135). Even then, women in Germany were not allowed to pursue higher education. This all shows that prohibitive laws were in effect for many years after female suffrage was gained. In addition, the traditional gender hierarchies in Greece were still held in place despite the involvement of women in national politics. Men still held most of the decision-making power (Paletschek, 264), which explains why there was little resistance against women's exclusion from citizenship after the proclamation of independence. Overall, the progress towards women's full citizenship and political participation was slow in the 20th century.

Text 5 has a strong first sentence that focuses the paragraph on women's lack of success gaining citizenship within the context of the women's movement. Thus, it positions the reader as someone who might think that achieving suffrage meant everything was perfect for women. It follows this point with details and quotations from multiple sources and concludes with a link back to the main point of the paragraph. The entire paragraph stays focused on women's citizenship, and the author comments on evidence with phrases like "which explains." The student uses words like "only" that help establish the restricted scope of women's rights, and *counter-expectational* words like "even then" and "despite" and "still" that help the writer position the reader consistently as someone who would agree that these pieces of evidence would be surprising for a reader who had believed that achieving suffrage equaled far-reaching success.

While argumentative writing across disciplines can have different conventions for integrating and managing outside voices, all argumentative writing requires the effective use of interpersonal resources. By making students aware of these resources and helping them consider their potential effects, we can help them overcome the challenge discussed in this section and increase their ability to respond to the expectations of argument in any of their university writing assignments.

3. How Can We Help Students With This Challenge?

3.1. The Engagement Framework

We use the Engagement framework (Martin & White, 2005) to help students understand how to integrate outside voices to support their argument, use language to establish and maintain a consistent position, and anticipate and manage the reader's expectations. This framework is based on a dialogic conceptualization of writing: that is, writers are entering a conversation with all others who have written about the same topic, and they are in a dialog with their potential readers. Accordingly, small language choices that writers make reveal how they anticipate the audience will react to the statements put forth; these choices position the reader in a certain way. In arguments, writers can use these language choices strategically to align the reader to their perspective, in other words, to be more persuasive.

According to the Engagement framework, there are two basic types of statements that writers make:

- **single-voiced** statements that present information as fact; the writer's perspective is the only perspective
- **multi-voiced** statements that present information as debatable; the writer acknowledges different perspectives and presents their perspective as an interpretation that needs to be argued for

Single-voiced statements typically use verbs in the simple present or past tense, indicating that the writer does not anticipate disagreement from the reader (e.g., *The sky is blue*). In other words, these statements are noncontroversial. They suggest that statement is a fact, or something the writer wants to be taken as a fact.

Multi-voiced statements can perform two different functions. They can expand the dialog by acknowledging or inviting other perspectives, or narrow the dialog by demonstrating awareness of other perspectives while bringing the reader away from these toward the writer's perspective.

Table 5.1 shows different types of single-voiced and multi-voiced statements that can be used in arguments. It is important to emphasize to students that arguments make use of single-voiced and multi-voiced statements. If students have an entire paragraph of single-voiced statements, it means they are presenting information as *factual*, not as something that needs to be *argued*.

Table 5.1: Explanations and Illustrations of Engagement Moves Found in Student Writing

Interpersonal resources	Engagement move	Description	Rhetorical effect	Example	Possible discourse markers
Single-voiced	Bare assertion	Writer represents the statement to be factual or noncontroversial.	Aligns a reader who agrees; dis-aligns a reader who does not agree.	The war began in 1941.	Non-modalized verb use (e.g., simple present or simple past tense)
Multi-voiced *dialogic expansion*	Modality	Writer keeps alternative perspectives in play in a context where likelihood of disagreement is high.	Avoids alienating the reader by allowing room for multiple voices or interpretations.	This can <u>perhaps</u> also mean that women were less literate than men.	Perhaps Possibly May
	Acknowledge	Writer uses a framing device to bring an external voice into the text, yet without displaying an overt attitude toward the external perspective.	Demonstrates interaction with another voice, broadening the range of perspectives on the topic.	<u>A law from Hammurabi's states</u>, "if a man takes a woman as a wife . . .	According to . . . X suggests . . . X says . . .
Dialogic narrowing	Endorse	Writer references an outside source and indicates support for the ideas or conclusions of the source text/ author.	May strengthen the writer's argument by providing a particular interpretation of the sourced evidence.	[direct or indirect reference to the source text]. <u>This depicts that</u> the Babylonian women had no right to freedom of choice.	X proves . . . X shows . . . X demonstrates . . .
	Pronounce	Writer inserts own voice explicitly into the text.	Emphasizes the point being made and rejects alternative perspectives.	<u>. . . I believe that</u> Hammurabi's code was fair with women . . .	The fact is . . . I contend that . . . Indeed . . .

(Continued)

Table 5.1: (Cont.)

Interpersonal resources	Engagement move	Description	Rhetorical effect	Example	Possible discourse markers
	Deny	Writer rejects the perspective that is projected onto the reader.	May be confrontational (dis-aligning) or corrective (aligning).	They were <u>not</u> seen as equally as men . . . . Men and women were <u>not</u> treated fully and genuinely.	No Did not Never
	Counter	Writer advances a perspective that is contrary to typical expectations.	Often positions the reader as sharing the writer's surprise at the counter-expectational case (aligning).	Every single law is addressed to the men . . . <u>even</u> when the laws are closely referring to female issues.	Yet But Even
Expanding-Narrowing	Attribute-Endorse	Writer brings in the source text to introduce evidence, then articulates how that evidence supports the writer's position.	Allows the reader to see sourced evidence and its relevance to the argument.	According to the author, "The plague killed thousands of people before the arrival of the opposing army." This shows that the war was one of several causes for the population decline.	According to . . . " . . . " This shows . . . The author states . . . " . . . " This means . . .
	Concede-Counter	Writer anticipates resistance from the reader, suggests that having an opposing perspective is understandable, then explains why it does not hold to be true.	Aligns the reader to the speaker's position.	There are <u>some</u> rights given when "a man wishes to separate from a woman" . . . . <u>Although even</u> this is for the sole reason that the woman can bring up the children, not for her own benefit.	Admittedly . . . + but . . . While . . . + still . . . Sure . . . + however . . .

Note: Descriptions are adapted from Martin and White (2005).

3.2. The Big Effects of Small Choices on the Reader-Writer Relationship

The Engagement framework helps students understand that small choices can have big effects on the reader. For example, it can help them consider the rhetorical effect of similar sentences with key differences:

1. *Gentrification is the reason prices are high.*
2. *Gentrification may be the reason prices are high.*
3. It is clear that *gentrification is the reason that prices are high.*

Students usually are quick to understand that the small change from sentence 1 to sentence 2, the use of *modality*, opens the dialog in a way that has a softer effect on a reader who might disagree; and that the difference between sentence 2 and sentence 3, a *narrowing* choice, changes the rhetorical effect: the *pronounce* move shrinks the dialogic space by emphasizing the point being made and implicitly rejecting alternatives.

The Engagement framework helps explain other choices that have subtler, but important, effects. For example, consider the implications of this sentence: *I enjoyed all of my classes today, even Professor Mitchell's.* Here, the word "even" signals that this is a counter-expectational case. In other words, it signals that the writer and reader agree that usually his class is not enjoyable. Examples like this explain how small choices reveal how the writer positions the reader, and how the writer estimates the reader's perspective on the topic at hand.

We need to emphasize to students that experienced writers use expanding and narrowing moves in combination throughout their argumentative paragraphs, creating a strategic mix that guides the reader toward their perspective. By allowing room for multiple perspectives, writers avoid alienating a potentially resistant reader who may not readily agree with the argument.

One common way of combining expanding and narrowing moves is Attribute-Endorse. For example: *According to Lareau (2014), "Middle-class young adults appeared to have more success at gaining individualized accommodation than did working-class or poor young adults" (p. 6.) This shows that the cultural capital that had been developed in the children of middle-class homes was still paying dividends when they were adults.* With this combination, writers can introduce an author or source, quote directly from it, then explain the quote's relevance as evidence for the claim. By referring to the author and including a direct quotation

(*According to . . .*), writers show that this is a perspective shared by others. By explaining or linking the quotation to the claim (*this shows . . .*), writers narrow the dialog, limiting the range of possible reasons for including the quote to precisely the one they are aiming for.

Another common way of combining expanding and narrowing moves is Concede-Counter. For example: *Although it might seem like an inconsequential aspect of daily life, Lareau (2003) shows how parent-child arguments about what to eat for dinner provide the child with the confidence to be more assertive with authorities in institutional settings.* With this combination, the writer opens the dialogic space by conceding to an opposing point of view (*Although it* **might seem** *. . .*), then narrows the space by countering the conceded viewpoint. By conceding that it is understandable that someone might interpret things one way, but then providing reasons why that interpretation would be incorrect in this instance, writers show the reader that they are accounting for multiple possible interpretations before settling on the one being argued for. This move might make a resistant reader more receptive to the argument being made.

If writers neglect to show how a quote relates to their claim or to counter a conceded point, then they leave the dialog open when they should have narrowed it to bring the reader closer to their perspective. Thus, with its dialogic conceptualization of writing, the Engagement framework provides a rationale for moves that we want to see in our students' writing and the language needed to make these moves. From this perspective, we can avoid giving students prescriptive advice (*don't end the paragraph with a quotation*) and leverage the dialogic understanding of writing to help them understand why certain choices are more or less effective (*when you end the paragraph with a quotation, you are leaving the dialog open; you are letting the author have the last word and leaving it up the reader to interpret it, rather than narrowing the dialog so that the reader understands how the author's idea furthers your argument*).

4. Lessons

4.1. Distinguishing Between Single- and Multi-Voiced Texts

We suggest introducing Engagement resources by helping students understand the difference between a single-voiced and multi-voiced text. To do

Engagement 97

this, start by providing examples of each type of text and ask students to note any differences between them. Examples 1 and 2 below show this difference.

Example 1	Example 2
The treatment of women in ancient Babylon was unfair. The women suffered a lot. The laws created different punishments for men and women. The wife received benefits when there were children involved.	By analyzing Hammurabi's Code, it becomes clear that the treatment of women in ancient Babylon was unfair compared to men. Code 24 states, " . . . " This indicates how skewed the laws were towards the benefit of men. Even laws like Code 28 that seem to benefit women were actually designed to protect children.

By asking students to contrast these examples that have similar overall content, you can help them see the importance of integrating outside voices and imagining a reader who needs to be persuaded. You can help students identify the use of the source text in Example 2 to contextualize the assertion that women were treated unfairly and to bring in direct evidence. Then, you can help them contrast this with Example 1, where there is no reference to the source text to support the assertions being made. Using Example 2, you can then begin to use metalanguage from Engagement, discussing the incorporation of the source text in terms of expanding the dialog by *acknowledging* the source text (*Code 24 states*) and quoting from it, and then narrowing the dialog with an *endorse* move that articulates how the quote supports the writer's argument (*This indicates*), and thus brings the reader closer to the writer's perspective. You can also point out the counter-expectational "even" that anticipates a potential exception to the claim being advanced and uses modality (*seem*) to open dialogic space for this perspective before pointing out that this evidence is "actually" in line with the claim. These resources allow students to present an analysis of their evidence, formulate *reasons* to explain *why* they chose certain quotes, and assert how the evidence supports their claims.

After contrasting the first two examples, ask students to look for differences between Example 3 and Example 4. Draw their attention to how Example 4 creates a better balance between the writer's voice and the voice of the source text, keeping the author in focus while making claims about the text.

Example 3	Example 4
Zukin argues that authenticity in a city is found in social diversity. This happens when new residents move in without making things too expensive for the long-time residents who give the place its character. Too often policy makers equate authenticity with preservation of historic buildings while ignoring the human element. They ignore the longtime residents and everything gets replaced by what is trendy and new. Policies that maintain social diversity create situations where people of high-income shop in international brands stores in the same neighborhood where middle- and low-income residents choose to shop in a mom-and-pop business. Neighbors are of different ethnicities, demand in stores is diversified, two different qualities of buildings exist opposite side of each other, and a public park has kids of different social classes playing together.	Zukin argues that authenticity in a city is found in social diversity. She suggests that this happens when new residents move in without making things too expensive for the longtime residents who give the place its character: "the movement of rich, well-educated folks [displace] the gentry into lower-class neighborhoods, and the higher property values that follow them, transforming a 'declining' district into an expensive neighborhood with historic or hipster charm" (p. 8). This hipster charm is not enough to make a neighborhood authentic; when policy makers equate authenticity with preservation of historic buildings, they ignore the longtime residents, and everything gets replaced by what is trendy and new. Zukin provides examples of policies that have been implemented to maintain social diversity, showing how they create situations where people of high-income shop in international brands stores in the same neighborhood where middle- and low-income residents choose to shop in a mom-and-pop business. By maintaining this social diversity, where people of different economic and social backgrounds frequent the same spaces, the authenticity of the place can be preserved.

It is important to emphasize to students that there is a lot of variety in how effective writers combine Engagement resources and there is not one correct way of doing so. Teaching them about these resources is valuable so that they have a meta-awareness of what subtle choices imply about the writer-reader relationship.

4.2. Identifying Engagement Resources

Once the students have been introduced to the Engagement framework, have them try to identify the resources used in the paragraph in Table 5.2. You can give them the paragraph with the resources in bold or see how many they can identify in an unmarked version of the paragraph (Text 4

Engagement 99

in Section 2). Once they have attempted to identify the resources on their own, provide them with the fully annotated version of the text. Ask them to consider these questions:

1. How does the writer's decision to start with a concede-counter move affect the rest of the paragraph?
2. How does the writer's decision to start with a concede-counter move relate to the position asserted in the thesis and the previous paragraph?
3. What do the writer's choices imply about the imagined reader's perspective on the success of the women's movement?

Table 5.2: Activity for Identifying Engagement Resources in an Analytical Argument

Prompt and student text	Engagement resources
Prompt: To what extent was the women's movement successful in Europe in the early 20th century?	
Thesis: The women's movement in Europe had mixed success in Europe in the early 20th century.	
Body Paragraph 1: The women's movement succeeded in achieving suffrage in most European countries . . .	
Body Paragraph 2: **Although** women achieved suffrage, women's fight for citizenship was **not as successful** in Europe during the early 20th century.	Concede-Counter
According to Ruiz and Rubio-Marín, "the political status of women cannot be fully understood without considering all aspects of citizenship" (136). **This means** that the right to vote	Attribute-Endorse
did not guarantee full political participation for many women.	Counter
For example, after women's suffrage began, in most European countries, women were only allowed to partici-pate in political activities if they were citizens, and their only way to express their political opinions was through organizational work, journalism, and community activism.	Counter
Furthermore, **according to Ruiz and Rubio-Marín**, German women automatically lost their citizenship if they married a foreigner until 1953, and these women were unable to pass citizenship to their children until the decision of the German Federal Constitutional Court in 1974 (135).	Attribute

(Continued)

ANALYSIS AND ARGUMENT IN FIRST-YEAR WRITING AND BEYOND

Table 5.2: (Cont.)

Even then, women in Germany **were not allowed** to pursue higher education.	Counter
This all shows that prohibitive laws were in effect for many years after female suffrage was gained.	Endorse
In addition, the traditional gender hierarchies in Greece were still held in place **despite** the involvement of women in national politics.	Counter
Men still held most of the decision-making power **(Paletschek, 264), which explains** why there was little resistance against women's exclusion from citizenship after the proclamation of independence.	Attribute-Endorse
Overall, the progress towards women's full citizenship and political participation was slow in the 20th century.	Single-voiced

With these questions, guide the students toward understanding how the use of the *concede-counter* move to open the paragraph creates the need for multiple *counter* moves throughout the paragraph. With that opening move, the writer is positioning the reader as someone who might think that the success of the suffrage movement meant the women's movement was completely successful, so the writer continues providing evidence to demonstrate how the movement's success was limited in other ways. This also helps further the thesis and develop the argument that success was mixed after having provided evidence of success in the previous paragraph. Despite this overall approach toward narrowing the dialogic space away from this perspective, the writer does mix in *attribute* moves to bring in authoritative voices to support the argument, combining them with *endorse* moves to explain their significance. The paragraph concludes with a single-voiced statement that reinforces the paragraph's overall claim. In this way, the writer implies that sufficient evidence has been provided to warrant a bare assertion that the reader will agree with.

You can also give the students paragraphs where the authorial voices are more dominant to show them how these resources can work similarly when the rhetorical situation is slightly different. In our first-year writing classroom, students have to synthesize the perspectives of several authors on the role of cultural and social capital in facilitating social class mobility. Thus, the students have to show how multiple authors' perspectives connect to support a shared claim.

Have students try to identify the resources used in the paragraph in Table 5.3. You can give them the paragraph with the resources in bold or

Engagement 101

see how many they can identify in an unmarked version of the paragraph. Ask them to consider these questions:

1. How does the expectation to synthesize other perspectives affect the writer-reader interaction?
2. How does the text's author use the voices of the scholarly research to open and narrow the dialog?
3. Where do we see the text's author's voice?

Table 5.3: Activity for Identifying Engagement Resources in an Analytical Synthesis

Student text	Engagement resources
The cultural capital that children develop through their daily experiences provides wealthier children with an advantage that facilitates social class mobility. Specifically, wealthier children develop interactional styles that are valued when speaking with authority figures in institutional settings.	Single-voiced
For example, **Lareau (2003) provides evidence** that children in wealthier homes are encouraged to reason and argue with their parents about things like what the family should eat for dinner.	Endorse
Although it might appear to be an inconsequential aspect of daily life, **Lareau shows** how such parent-child arguments provide the child with the confidence to be assertive with authorities in institutional settings, such as asking for help from a teacher or being inquisitive with a doctor during a medical visit.	Concede-Counter
Khan (2010) documents a similar phenomenon in his ethnography of an elite boarding school where the wealthier students tacitly understood how the social setting influenced how they should interact with their teachers.	Endorse
According to Khan, the wealthier students would joke with him when visiting his apartment while still being respectful but then show much more deference and formality towards him in the classroom.	Attribute
He emphasizes how this skill is useful for navigating social situations with their future bosses in interactions outside of work.	Endorse
Taken together, **this evidence shows** how valuable cultural capital developed during childhood creates significant advantages for wealthier children throughout their lives.	Endorse

102   ANALYSIS AND ARGUMENT IN FIRST-YEAR WRITING AND BEYOND

With these questions, guide the students toward understanding how a synthesis of other perspectives is a rhetorical situation where the writer is unlikely to encounter a resistant reader. For this reason, this paragraph has more narrowing moves than opening ones. If a reader disagrees with some aspect of this paragraph, it is because they know these texts and detect an inaccurate portrayal, a case in which no amount of interactive resources would be helpful.

You can then help the students see how the same types of moves that they analyzed in the previous paragraph appear here, but in this case it is the writer using the scholarly authors to bring in evidence and explain what it means for the paragraph's overall point. Finally, you can encourage them to consider the effect of the single-voiced statements at the beginning of the paragraph. While the writer's voice is implicit throughout the text—selecting, interpreting, and presenting information—it is in these opening sentences where the writer's voice is most clearly present.

4.3. Revising Texts Using Engagement Resources to Make Them More Effective

We suggest working with some examples that exhibit challenges managing the reader's expectations. You can work with texts from your previous classes by taking an effective paragraph and removing some of the effective uses of Engagement resources and asking students to identify places where the text could bring in support from an author, explain the significance of a quote, or anticipate and refute a counter argument. Or you can take a paragraph a student has written that exhibits some of the challenges discussed in this chapter and work together as a class to point out what could be improved and revise it as a group.

We think that students gain more from this exercise if they work with texts that have familiar content. It will be easier for them to supply ideas for improvement if they are already involved in the "dialog" you want them to improve. However, you can also use the examples from this chapter. For example, give students Text 3 from Section 2 with these instructions:

> *This paragraph lacks a clear coherent claim. As a result, it positions the reader inconsistently and uses too many counter moves. Revise the paragraph to support the following claim: The suffrage movement in Europe was a combination of bottom-up efforts and top-down policies that developed at an uneven pace in different countries.*

5. Concluding Remarks

The language-focused tools presented in this chapter can be applied to genres in many contexts that require analytical and argumentative writing. Instructors can examine genres they teach to uncover valued ways of reasoning and building knowledge. They can explore with students how different rhetorical situations require managing reader expectations in different ways. We have found that making students aware of writing as a dialog can be an important first step. Then, providing them with examples of the big effects of small rhetorical choices can help them toward purposeful writing that consistently and effectively moves the reader toward their position.

Reference

Martin, J. R., & White, P. R. R. (2005). *The language of evaluation*. Palgrave Macmillan.

CHAPTER 6

Justification: Resources for Justifying a Position Among Alternatives

1. What Is the Expectation and What Is the Challenge for Students?

In genres across the curriculum, students are expected to discuss alternatives and to maintain a consistent stance while arguing for a preferred position (e.g., a solution) among alternatives.

However, our research (Pessoa et al., 2023) shows that students face difficulties using evaluative resources to justify a position among alternatives. Many students present alternatives, list their advantages and disadvantages, but neglect to take up an assignment's instruction to *argue* for the better alternative by, for example, evaluating it more positively through comparative reasoning or by countering its drawbacks. Students are sometimes so focused on discussing alternatives that they neglect to take a position in favor of one perspective. As a result, students lose track of their argument, weighing perspectives equally or providing inadequate reasoning for choosing one perspective over the other(s).

In this chapter, we present resources for justifying a position among alternatives.

2. What Does the Challenge Look Like in First-Year Writing and in Writing in the Disciplines?

In first-year writing courses it is common for students to be assigned writing prompts that invite multiple perspectives. A common assignment in

Justification: Resources for Justifying a Position Among Alternatives 105

first-year writing courses (and in the disciplines) is the problem-solution paper. In a problem-solution paper, students have to identify and analyze a specific problem in-depth and propose a viable solution or set of solutions to address it. In offering one or more potential solutions to the problem, students are expected to:

- describe each solution in detail, explaining how it addresses the causes and consequences of the problem;
- support the proposed solutions with evidence, examples, and logical reasoning;
- evaluate the feasibility and potential effectiveness of each proposed solution;
- consider any potential drawbacks, limitations, or challenges associated with implementing the solutions;
- compare and contrast the different solutions to highlight their strengths and weaknesses; and
- argue for one solution among the alternative solutions.

Table 6.1 provides examples of such prompts.

Table 6.1: Writing Prompts That Invite Multiple Perspectives in First-Year Writing Courses

1. Discuss a specific environmental problem in your local community and propose practical solutions to address it. Provide a persuasive argument for why a specific solution is the best alternative.
2. Identify the main causes and consequences of poverty in your country and propose effective strategies to alleviate it. Provide a persuasive argument for what the best strategy is.
3. Analyze the challenges associated with healthcare accessibility in urban areas and suggest measures to improve access for marginalized populations. Provide a persuasive argument that states what the best strategy is.
4. Examine the issue of food insecurity among college students and propose initiatives that universities can implement to combat this problem.
5. Explore the impact of social media on mental health and suggest strategies for promoting a healthier online environment.
6. Identify the main causes and effects of traffic congestion in your city and propose feasible solutions to alleviate the problem.
7. Analyze the issue of bullying in schools and propose comprehensive anti-bullying strategies to ensure a safe and inclusive learning environment.
8. Discuss the problem of limited access to clean drinking water in developing countries and propose innovative solutions to ensure safe and affordable water sources.
9. Discuss the advantages and disadvantages of majoring in the humanities versus majoring in science. Which is the better alternative? Provide a persuasive argument.

In disciplines such as information systems, business administration, and management programs, students are often given assignments that require them to consider multiple solutions to a problem. For example, at our institution, students majoring in information systems complete a software development project at the end of their third year. As a team, students work with a real client to design, build, and deliver an information systems sustainable solution that fits the client's objectives, organizational constraints, and capabilities. In the proposal and the report for the client, students describe at least two alternative solutions to address their client's problem, reflect on the advantages and disadvantages of each alternative solution, and justify why the chosen solution is the best alternative (see Table 6.2 for a more detailed description of the assignment prompt).

In an organizational behavior course that students majoring in business administration take at our institution, students have to write a Case Analysis where they evaluate a company through an organizational behavior lens (i.e., course concepts, insights, and frameworks). Based on their analysis, they are expected to provide two recommendations for improving the company's organizational behavior, to consider the advantages and disadvantages of each of the two recommended options, and to argue for the best recommendation (see Table 6.2 for a more detailed description of the assignment prompt).

Table 6.2: Writing Prompts That Invite Multiple Perspectives in Disciplinary Courses

Discipline: Information Systems
Problem Analysis
Given the background of your partner organization, this section should identify and describe the problem(s) facing the organization for which your assistance was requested and the reason(s) why it is important to solve this/these problem(s). Discuss any solutions that have been considered by the client prior to your project and the pitfalls of those proposed solutions. Explain how solving the problem generates value to the client from an organizational or business perspective (e.g., improved quality of service, better products, or return on investment).
Solution
1. Solution Alternatives
Describe what alternative solutions exist (at least two) to address the problem described earlier, and evaluate these solutions. In your evaluation, for each alternative solution, reflect on advantages and disadvantages.

Justification: Resources for Justifying a Position Among Alternatives 107

Table 6.2: (Cont.)

2. Chosen Alternative & Justification Provide a persuasive argument for why the chosen solution is the best alternative. Clarify the objectives, purpose, or scope of your proposed solution. Explain how the chosen solution aligns with the client's resources and competencies. **Discipline: Organizational Behavior** 1. What actionable options are available for resolving the key problem/opportunity? Provide two recommended options. 2. What are the advantages and disadvantages of each of the two recommended options? 3. What is the best recommendation? Why? Argue for this one recommended approach and explain why you recommend this approach for your case.

In assignments like the ones in Table 6.2, the student is often expected to make a claim about how to fix a company's problems and support the claim with reasoning. In supporting their claim for a particular recommendation, students are often asked to consider alternatives as "a key step towards formulation of recommendations for action which are crucial elements" (Nathan, 2016, p. 2) in the genre.

In our work scaffolding this type of writing, we have observed that sometimes students are so focused on providing alternative solutions that they neglect to take a position on or support a preferred recommendation. As a result, students lose track of their argument, weighing each solution equally or providing inadequate reasoning for choosing one perspective over the other(s).

Sample Texts 1 and 2 show recommendations sections where the writers display a lack of awareness of the need to *argue* for the better alternative. The two examples are based on responses to the organizational behavior Case Analysis assignment shown in Table 6.2.

SAMPLE 1: An Argumentatively Underdeveloped Recommendations Section

Another recommendation that Zappos can use to turn its potential problem into an opportunity is educating its employees on misbehavior . . . . Thus, with employee knowledge, cost would decrease, resulting in profit increase.

While employee misbehavior education could decrease employee turnover and increase profit, it is costly and time-consuming. Successful companies like Microsoft spend $82 per learning hour on average. This is relatively expensive, especially that not all employees take these education sessions seriously (i.e., some employees do not attend). Another drawback is that this recommendation is time-consuming-that is, the time that gets spent on these sessions could be utilized on completing job tasks, as an

108   ANALYSIS AND ARGUMENT IN FIRST-YEAR WRITING AND BEYOND

example. Zappos is recommended to use employee misbehavior education as a tool to turn its anticipated problem into an opportunity. This is because educating employees on misbehavior would have an immediate positive effect on the company's financial statements, as shown above.

SAMPLE 2: A Recommendations Section With no Comparative Argument or Countering of Drawbacks

The first recommendation is for Ford to apply the first step of Kotter's 8-step change model (2014), by creating a *sense of urgency* since it addresses the issue of *organizational culture* . . .

The advantages of this recommendation are there will be a faster, more productive change at Ford and higher motivation. Since the company is in a poor position, an urgent change is required, and employees may be more acceptable towards the 24-hour rule which would drive Ford's output towards problem solving. Employees may feel more involved so a better culture is created, and their motivation can increase, and they may be more satisfied with the leadership style. On the other hand, the disadvantage of this recommendation is because there needs to be a fast change, there might be stress amongst employees. It may create a tense organizational culture that can build up anxiety in the workplace for employees. . . .

The best recommended approach for Ford is to apply the first step of Kotter's 8-step change model (2014), by creating a sense of urgency. It will address the problem of organizational culture, by showing employees the need for fast change. Engaging employees in the decision of change can create trust between the employees of Ford and the new CEO. With this approach, employees may be more accepting toward change, and their productivity and efficiency can increase, so it can create a positive organizational culture and solve the issue of leadership. Hence, this approach is recommended for Ford Motor Company as it would increase the productivity and motivation of employees, as well as increase their efficiency.

In Sample 1, the student states that a potential solution to alleviate Zappos's problems is to conduct *employee misbehavior education*. After stating the benefits of this potential solution (e.g., *cost would decrease, resulting in profit increase*), the writer states that *While employee misbehavior education could decrease employee turnover and increase profit, it is costly and time-consuming*. This statement moves the reader away from the writer's ultimate position; rather than referring to the disadvantages

Justification: Resources for Justifying a Position Among Alternatives   109

and conceding that they are worthy of consideration before ultimately rejecting them, the writer concedes that the solution has benefits, but then counters that it is *costly and time-consuming*. After providing evidence for that claim, they endorse the same recommendation they just negatively evaluated, with only one sentence of justification and no countering of the negatives they referred to. The justification is very general (*positive effect on the company's financial statement, as shown above*), referring the reader to the prior text instead of revisiting evidence or using a comparison to support a claim about this solution being the better of the two.

In Sample 2, the student asserts that the first recommendation is the best (*The best recommended approach for Ford is to apply the first step of Kotter's 8-step change model . . .*) but offers no comparative support to justify their comparative claim. The student only provides restatements of the positive evaluations of the first alternative solution with no mention of the second alternative solution. Furthermore, the student does not counter the negative evaluations of the disadvantages of their recommended solution. Thus, the reader is left to wonder why this recommendation is better than the other, and why the company should not be overly concerned with the stated disadvantages this recommendation might have or if they could be mitigated in some way. Clearly, this student had the inclination to provide a relatively substantial justification of their preferred recommendation but did not go beyond repeating the positive effects of their selection.

Given these challenges, how can writers effectively justify a position among alternatives? And how can teachers help their students maintain a consistent stance while arguing for a preferred position among alternatives?

3. What Resources Can We Use to Address the Challenge?

To help students justify a position among alternatives, we show students how writing an effective Discussion genre can help them achieve their persuasive purpose. Within Systemic Functional Linguistics (SFL), Discussions, which are part of the Argument genre family, are organized around multiple positions (multi-sided), introducing several perspectives

110 ANALYSIS AND ARGUMENT IN FIRST-YEAR WRITING AND BEYOND

on an issue, and evaluating them positively or negatively (Coffin, 1996, 2006; Martin & Rose, 2008). Discussions include:

- an Issue stage that introduces the aim of the whole section and orients the reader to what will be discussed;
- Perspective stages that neutrally discuss the advantages and disadvantages of two different positions or steer the reader toward one side by strategically evaluating arguments and evidence; and
- a final Resolution stage that provides a justification for the position the author sides with.

Having a well-developed Resolution is vital for the Discussion genre, particularly in texts that remain neutral in the Perspective stages. Let us go back to Sample Text 1, which we presented in the previous section. In Table 6.3 below we show an annotated version of this text.

Table 6.3: An Argumentatively Underdeveloped Resolution Stage

PERSPECTIVE 2
Another recommendation that Zappos can use to turn its potential problem into an opportunity is educating its employees on misbehavior . . . . Thus, with employee knowledge, cost would decrease, resulting in profit increase.

While employee misbehavior education could decrease employee turnover and increase profit, it is costly and time-consuming. Successful companies like Microsoft spend $82 per learning hour on average. This is relatively expensive, especially that not all employees take these education sessions seriously (i.e., some employees do not attend). Another drawback is that this recommendation is time-consuming-that is, the time that gets spent on these sessions could be utilized on completing job tasks, as an example. RESOLUTION Zappos is recommended to use employee misbehavior education as a tool to turn its anticipated problem into an opportunity. This is because educating employees on misbehavior would have an immediate positive effect on the company's financial statements, as shown above.

In this annotated version of the text, we see that the student only provides two sentences of Resolution, which are tacked on to the end of the final paragraph of Perspective 2, one that is focused on the disadvantages of one of the alternative solutions (*educating Zappos' employees on misbehavior*). The student begins this paragraph with a concede-counter move that moves the reader away from their ultimate position (*While employee misbehavior education . . . , it is costly and time-consuming*). Instead of simply presenting the disadvantages and acknowledging their validity before ultimately rejecting them, the student acknowledges the benefits of the proposed solution but counters that it is expensive and time-consuming. Subsequently, they provide evidence to support this claim

Justification: Resources for Justifying a Position Among Alternatives 111

(*Successful companies like Microsoft spend $82 per learning hour on average. This is relatively expensive . . .*). Surprisingly, despite the negative evaluation, they then endorse the same recommendation, but with only a single sentence of justification and without addressing the aforementioned drawbacks. The justification is quite general, as it refers the reader back to the prior text (highlighting the positive effect on the company's financial statement) instead of revisiting the evidence or making a comparison to support the claim that this solution is superior to the alternative.

Given that assignment guidelines usually ask students to argue for one of two proposed solutions, we also draw on Engagement (Martin & White, 2005) to help students effectively establish a consistent evaluative position and align the reader to it by:

- entertaining multiple perspectives through the use of modality to avoid alienating the reader (e.g., the company *can* do X vs. the company *must* do X);
- citing authoritative outside voices to support a course of action (e.g., *a study conducted by Wanberg & Mueller [2000] noted that*);
- using concede-counter moves to align a potentially resistant reader (e.g., *while* solution 1 has clear strengths . . . , solution 2 is *still* the best choice . . .); and
- using counter moves that narrow the range of acceptable positions to align the reader with the writer's stated position (e.g., Solution 2 has several disadvantages . . . . *However*, we recommend solution 2 . . .).

The lessons that follow show how we can help students write effective persuasive recommendations that maintain a consistent stance while arguing for a preferred solution among alternatives.

4. Lessons

4.1. Deconstructing Sample Texts to Show How to Meet Genre Expectations

To help students write effective persuasive texts, we suggest deconstructing sample texts to call students' attention to how the expectation of justifying a position among alternatives can be met by writing an effective Discussion genre that includes the following stages: Issue, Perspectives, and Resolution. As stated earlier, the Issue stage introduces the aim of the whole section and orients the reader to what will be discussed; Perspective stages neutrally discuss the advantages and disadvantages of two different positions or steer the reader toward one side by strategically evaluating arguments and evidence throughout the Perspective stages (Coffin, 2006); and the Resolution stage provides a justification for the position the author sides with.

Table 6.4 provides an example of a prototypical Discussion that has well-supported Perspective stages and substantial reasoning that supports the student's chosen solution. The examples we present in this section are based on responses to a Case Analysis assignment assigned in an organizational behavior course that asked the following:

1. What actionable options are available for resolving the key problem/ opportunity? Provide two recommended options.
2. What are the advantages and disadvantages of each of the two recommended options?
3. What is the best recommendation? Why? Argue for this one recommended approach and explain why you recommend this approach for your case.

Using the text in Table 6.4 as a sample, engage students in analyzing the text using guiding questions such as the following:

1. How is the text organized?
2. What is the focus of each paragraph?
3. How do the paragraphs relate to each other?
4. What are some of the language choices that tell you about the text's structure?

Table 6.4: A Prototypical Discussion

ISSUE
Amazon's acquisition of Whole Foods Market was a financially sound step for both companies. Yet, a cultural clash occurred after the acquisition because leaders often neglect the organizational behavior related consequences of the decisions they make. To overcome this problem and seize the opportunity of a cultural merger, I offer two strategic actions that I believe will help Whole Foods Market effectively manage their people and maintain their organizational culture.

PERSPECTIVE 1
The first strategic action that can be implemented is to have a transformational leader. One of the problems caused by the merger was the difference in leadership styles, which is one of the main causes of the clash of organizational cultures. Schein (1985) highlighted the role of leaders . . . . It is then the leader's role to encourage the employees . . . . In Avolio

Justification: Resources for Justifying a Position Among Alternatives 113

Table 6.4: (Cont.)

and Bass's *Improving Organizational Effectiveness through Transformational Leadership* (2002), it was asserted that . . . . Therefore, one strategic action I suggest is one Bass and Avolio (2002) have introduced, which is conducting a Multifactor Leadership Questionnaire (MLQ) to test whether the leader, Mackey, is transformational or not and based on that the organization will implement changes.

Having or hiring transformational leaders is a good strategy to follow because studies have found . . . . Also, the MLQ is a good measurable way to test the efficiency of leaders. On the other hand, this strategy's drawback is . . .

PERSPECTIVE 2
The second strategic action is offering a cultural program in Whole Foods Market based on Kotter's model of change (1988). This strategy solves the overall problem of organizational culture clash by focusing on employees' adaptation to the new culture. Kotter's model covers . . . . This model is closely related to organizational behavior in a way that targets macro-level organizational theory; yet it also acts as an organizational development tool that serves as a three-dimensional linkage between individuals, groups and the organization (Stragalas, 2010). If Whole Foods implement Kotter's model of change, they will probably solve the problem of their employees' difficulty in adapting to a new organizational culture, a new leadership style and a new decision-making process.

Implementing Kotter's 8-step model of change has an advantage of being an easy process that provides precise description of the steps to take. It also values and emphasizes the importance of employees' acceptance which can increase their job satisfaction and thus help in how they adapt in a new culture. On the other hand, it has a disadvantage of being time consuming . . . . However, I believe the results this process yields are worth the time spent on it especially because it was tested in many organizations and the results were millions of dollars saved, turnaround time reduced, and revenue goals exceeded (Kotter inc., 2019). Thus, by implementing this process, Whole Foods would also increase its profits by enhancing its employees' job satisfaction.

RESOLUTION
To solve Whole Foods problem of an organizational culture clash, I recommend offering a cultural program based on Kotter's model of change because it focuses on the bigger picture. This strategy has a clear process with precise steps and focuses on the employees as a whole rather than just the leaders. Although it is time consuming, the employees' acceptance and thus improved motivation and performance will be worth the time spent.

It is important to show students how the writer of the text in Table 6.4 includes an Issue stage that reminds the reader of the main problem that needs to be addressed and forecasts that they will offer two solutions to address the problem. You can indicate how, for each Perspective stage, the writer includes two paragraphs: the first provides the recommendation in a generalized way, citing multiple disciplinary sources to justify its validity for solving this kind of problem in all contexts before arriving at the final sentence that suggests how it could be applied, or what effects it would likely have in this particular context; the second provides advantages and

114   ANALYSIS AND ARGUMENT IN FIRST-YEAR WRITING AND BEYOND

disadvantages of the solution. In these advantage/disadvantage paragraphs, show how the writer provides reasons for the positive and negative evaluations with causal connections (e.g., *is a good strategy . . . because*) or "cause within the clause" verbs (e.g., *can increase their job satisfaction*).

Then you can direct students' attention to Perspective 2, where the writer provides the second alternative solution. Explain how the writer counters the negative evaluations of the second alternative solution (*however*) through the use of causal reasoning (*worth the time spent . . . because*; *would increase its profits*) to explain why they are acceptable in the long term. This is an important move because it helps the writer align the reader toward their preferred solution; advantages and disadvantages are weighed equally, but then the balance between them is quickly offset. As Coffin (2006) notes in her description of the Discussion genre in history, rather than remaining completely neutral until the Resolution, "persuasive writers evaluate arguments and evidence throughout . . . to steer their readers toward accepting their final interpretation" (p. 86).

Once you have analyzed the Perspective stages with the students, direct their attention to the Resolution stage, where the writer provides reasoning for preferring the second recommendation with a logical relation of cause (*I recommend offering a cultural program based on Kotter's model of change because it focuses on the bigger picture*). The writer also revisits (a) disciplinary-based descriptions from the first paragraph of Perspective 2, and (b) positive evaluations from Perspective 2. The writer uses logical relations of comparison to juxtapose these positive evaluations with the solution offered in the Perspective 1 stage (*focuses on the employees as a whole rather than just the leaders*). The writer closes with a concede-counter move (*Although it is time consuming . . . will be worth the time spent*), revisiting the main disadvantage of the preferred solution before reiterating why the advantages outweigh it.

It is important for students to recognize how the writer succeeds in writing a Discussion with all the expected stages. They cite disciplinary knowledge to validate their solutions as appropriate for this type of problem, provide reasoning in support of their advantages and disadvantages when applied to the case, and give a comparative argument for their preferred solution that counters its drawbacks.

In comparison with the prototypical Discussion in Table 6.4, you can show students a different approach where the writer foregrounds the persuasive goal of arguing for one solution throughout the text. Table 6.5 illustrates this approach, presenting a possible recommendation in the first

Justification: Resources for Justifying a Position Among Alternatives   115

Perspective stage, acknowledging its positive aspects and then immediately countering them with drawbacks. This allows writers to create a space for arguing for the preferred recommendation (in response to the disadvantages of the first recommendation) in the second Perspective. Such a move shows an understanding of the need to foreground persuasion: the writer imagines a reader who needs to be aligned toward their perspective by rejecting one possible recommendation and convincing the reader to take action on the other. Table 6.5 shows an example of this move.

Table 6.5: A Persuasive Discussion

> **ISSUE**
> Based on the analysis, this section will propose two recommendations that can enable Whole Foods' leadership to reshape its labor-force workplace culture by shifting employee perceptions and reducing individual stress. Finally, one recommendation will be emphasized via an action plan followed by its anticipated results to conclude that the issue can be resolved if leadership follows necessary steps to reshape organizational culture at the lowest level.
>
> **PERSPECTIVE 1**
> To better align the Whole Foods labor-force workplace culture with that of Amazon's and reduce individual stress, Whole Foods leadership must re-shape employee perception and increase communication. To increase communication, Whole Foods leadership can implement Employee Suggestion Management Systems (ESMS) that directly delivers employee feedback to Whole Foods and Amazon leadership. One ESMS, termed *STARS*, has been considered generally successful in "reducing waste and increasing employee satisfaction" (Charron-Latour, Bassetto, & Pourmonet, 2017). . . . STARS directly enabled faster communication at all levels of organizations by successfully shifting to a "culture-centered improvement management method" (Charron-Latour et al., 2017, p. 180). Additionally, ... **However,** while the STARS system presented predominantly positive results, the authors note that STARS still posed general difficulties and scored low on allowing managers to "clearly identify operational objectives" and "engage employees," who often viewed the system as yet another task in their work (p. 189). **These limitations** may develop into issues that fail to re-shape employee perception because the workforce may maintain that they feel overtasked and overburdened with another system on top of the requirements of the OTS system.
>
> **PERSPECTIVE 2**
> **The limitations of the STARS system suggest another better-fitting, more sustainable solution** for Whole Foods leadership to reduce stress and reshape employee perception. Based on research in post-mergers organizational management and organizational change from *Mergers 101 (part two): training managers for culture, stress, and change challenges* (Appelbaum, Lefrancois, Tonna, & Shapiro, 2007), a more sustainable solution would be to adopt socialization techniques during workforce upsizing to reshape organizational culture . . . . In order to ensure the successful implementation of the strategy, it is important to first understand that the upsizing of the Whole Foods labor workforce requires a substantial expenditure with regards to human resources. Additionally, the effects of the

(Continued)

ANALYSIS AND ARGUMENT IN FIRST-YEAR WRITING AND BEYOND

Table 6.5: (Cont.)

solution may not be realized immediately because socialization requires a period of time in which new employees adjust and adapt to their new environment and culture. However, the benefits of a humanistic solution that truly enables leaders to reshape employee perceptions through an increased laborer workforce far outweigh a one-size-fits-all system solution such as STARS that is mandated upon an already-stressed workforce. First, increasing the labor workforce would enable Whole Foods leadership to delegate fewer tasks to each individual laborer. This directly ensures that the leadership can sufficiently create appropriate levels of stress—especially when fulfillment of one's necessary quota becomes much more feasible. It is reasonable to conclude that when labor-workers are assigned less tasks and complete their given tasks successfully, employee distress will decrease and negative perceptions towards the OTS system will become less extreme. In addition, and more importantly, the upsizing of the workforce brings in fresh, new attitudes free from the anchoring effects in perception (Thorsteinson, 2008) that prevailing employees have developed prior to the acquisition. Having fresh perspectives . . . . If Whole Foods leadership communicates a higher set of expectations for its new workforce, its new employees will be able to transfer this energy and excitement to prevailing employees in what would ultimately become a positive feedback loop. This positive feedback loop shifts employee perceptions to better align with Amazon leadership culture as an increased labor force simultaneously reduces the individual stress of laborers. In turn, decreased employee stress and successful socialization that cultivates a better-aligned culture with mutual organizational values fosters sustainable positive employee perceptions.

In examining the text in Table 6.5 with the students, you can help them see how it opens with an Issue stage that indicates that two recommendations will be proposed to address the problems associated with labor-force workplace culture. Although the two recommendations are not previewed, the reader perceives that one recommendation will be favored (*one recommendation will be emphasized via an action plan*). You can call your students' attention to how the writer could have previewed the two potential recommendations for the reader.

The next two paragraphs represent the two Perspectives to be discussed (*increase communication* and *workforce upsizing*). The writer uses Perspective 1 to show that this is not the favored recommendation, and Perspective 2 as the preferred recommendation in response to the limitations of the first recommendation. Despite some imperfections with word choice and ordering of information, this rhetorical approach shows awareness of a reader that needs to be persuaded of a course of action.

In Perspective 1 (*Whole Foods must re-shape employee perception and increase communication*), show how the choice of the high obligation modality *must* is misleading because it may cause the reader to understand this to be the recommendation that the writer favors, especially

Justification: Resources for Justifying a Position Among Alternatives   117

since, drawing on disciplinary knowledge, the writer then puts forward two arguments that positively evaluate the use of the STARS management system (e.g., *generally successful; faster communication*). However, the writer brings to light the disadvantages of the STARS system by using a concede-counter (*However, while the STARS system presented predominantly positive results, the authors note that STARS still posed general difficulties . . .*). The writer then uses a causal relationship to emphasize the potential negative impact of the STARS system on the employees (*These limitations may develop into issues . . . because the workforce . . .*). Thus, once the reader gets to the end of this paragraph, it becomes clear that Perspective 1 is not a preferred recommendation. The paragraph moves from positive to negative evaluations, but does not counter the negative evaluations, as the drawbacks of the first potential solution lead the reader directly to the preferred one.

In response to the limitations of the recommendation in Perspective 1, show students how Perspective 2 starts with a thesis that comparatively and favorably evaluates workforce upsizing as a better solution (*better-fitting* and *more sustainable*). The focus on workforce upsizing, although initially rather wordy and unclear, becomes more apparent when the student acknowledges its nuances and potential constraints and counters them with a move that previews the benefits of this recommendation in contrast to the first recommendation (*However, the benefits of a humanistic solution . . .*).

What follows are two paragraphs that emphasize the benefits of increasing the workforce at Whole Foods through only positive evaluations (e.g., *appropriate levels of stress; fresh, new attitudes*) with "cause within the clause" verbs (e.g., *this positive feedback loop shifts employee perceptions; reduces stress*) and conditional relations (*If Whole Foods leadership communicates a higher set of expectations for its new workforce . . .*).

It is important to discuss with students that the writer does not finish the recommendations section with a Resolution. Instead, in the last two sentences the writer repeats many of the same key words that were used throughout Perspective 2: *employee perceptions, leadership culture, increased labor force, reduces the individual stress of laborers, decreased employee stress, socialization culture,* and *employee perceptions.* You can explain how adding a separate Resolution stage would have been unnecessarily repetitive. A more effective approach could have been to save the nuances and potential constraints of the preferred solution (*the upsizing of the Whole Foods labor workforce requires a substantial expenditure with regards to human resources; the effects of the solution may not be realized immediately because . . .*) for the end of Perspective 2, using it as a Resolution that dismisses the potential drawbacks of the recommendation and provides a brief comparative argument (*However, the benefits . . . far outweigh a one-size-fits-all . . .*). You can engage in co-construction and collaboratively rewrite Perspective 2 and a Resolution.

Although we present examples from our own students' work, we encourage instructors to create their own samples with their students' texts. We also encourage instructors to use student texts with underdeveloped and unjustified Resolution stages or ineffective embedding of genres and discuss ways to improve the texts.

4.2. Strategies That Can Be Used to Justify the Benefits of a Preferred Option or Alternative

In addition to helping students write effective persuasive recommendations by providing examples of effective discussions to achieve a persuasive purpose, we suggest raising students' awareness of strategies that can be used to justify the benefits of a preferred alternative. Show students a list of strategies like the one in Table 6.6 to justify the benefits of a preferred alternative.

Table 6.6: Strategies to Justify the Benefits of a Preferred Option or Alternative

> • Arguing that a desired outcome **depends on following the option/alternative**
> e.g., *If Monoprix wants to be successful in Qatar, they will need to recognize that supermarkets in Qatar are different to those in France.*
> • **Comparing** the proposed solution to a different course of action
> e.g., *Gap might be able to avoid major controversy with its current vendor selection system, but negative publicity is much less likely with a partnership sourcing process.*
> • Using **benchmarking** to show how other companies have addressed a similar problem and how similar recommendations have been implemented in similar contexts
> e.g., *This approach has proved profitable in Apple, where the company increased productivity by 36% after implementing it.*
> • Quoting an **authority figure** (Donohue et al., 2009)
> e.g., *As Bryan Jackson, director of Toyota Motor Manufacturing UK, points out: "It's rather difficult to have a relationship with 1,000 suppliers."*

To help students identify these strategies in texts, ask them to read a sample recommendations section and identify the strategy that is being used to support the recommendation. Table 6.7 shows a sample activity.

Justification: Resources for Justifying a Position Among Alternatives 119

Table 6.7: Sample Activity for Students to Identify the Strategy That Is Being Used to Support a Recommendation

Read the following *Recommendations section*
Remember: The assignment guidelines state that your recommendations must be **evidence-based.** You need to support your recommendations with one or more of the following:
- a researched process—*What empirical studies show results that support your recommendation?*
- actions based on a theory—*How can OB theory help support the feasibility and desirability of your recommendation in this particular context?*
- benchmarking—*How have other companies addressed a similar problem? How have similar recommendations been implemented in similar contexts?*

1. Where in the text can you find examples of these? Please mark the sections where the writers refer to a researched process (RP), to actions based on a theory (ABT), and to benchmarking (BM).
2. Of the evidence that you identified in #1, which evidence is the most concrete and specific?

Sample Case Proposal: M University (MU)
[Recommendation Section Only]
4. Recommendations
Recent changes in the leadership at MU have led to a decrease in diversity, a change in priorities, and the adoption of a Telling Leadership style. These aspects of the new leadership, which do not seem to be aligned with the university's culture of inclusion and academic excellence, have negatively affected employee retention and motivation. Based on our assessment, we offer two strategic recommendations that we believe are efficient to address the current situation at MU.

Our first recommendation is that the senior leaders at MU implement a **Transformational Leadership Style** (Bass & Riggio, 2005). This style focuses on inspiring and motivating employees by creating a vision, setting high expectations, and providing support and guidance. Transformational leaders are known for their ability to articulate a compelling vision that inspires and motivates employees (Judge & Piccolo, 2004). By setting a clear direction and communicating a shared sense of purpose, MU can rally faculty and staff around common goals, fostering a sense of unity and commitment. A Transformational Leadership Style also recognizes and supports the unique needs and aspirations of each employee. By understanding the strengths and aspirations of faculty and staff, the senior leaders at MU can provide personalized development opportunities, mentorship, and support, promoting their growth and job satisfaction.

Although adopting a Transformational Leadership Style is certainly a viable solution for MU, it is important to consider that in a Transformational Leadership Style, the leader plays a central role in inspiring and motivating employees. This reliance on the leader's charisma and vision can create a dependency on their presence and guidance. If the leader is absent or leaves the organization, it may lead to a decline in employee motivation and a loss of direction (Judge & Piccolo, 2004). In addition, transformational leaders often set high expectations for their employees, aiming for ambitious goals and continuous improvement. While this can be inspiring, it may also create stress and pressure if employees feel overwhelmed or unable to meet these expectations. In some cases, employees may experience burnout or dissatisfaction if the goals set by the leader are perceived as unrealistic or unattainable.

(Continued)

Table 6.7: (Cont.)

To address the limitations associated with the Transformational Leadership Style and propose a more suitable and sustainable solution for MU, we advocate for the adoption of a **Participating Leadership Style** (Hersey & Blanchard, 1988). A Participating Leadership Style is characterized by a low task behavior and a high relationship behavior approach, focusing on problem-solving through active listening and collaborative engagement (Center for Leadership Studies, 2019). Leaders who embrace this style exhibit less directive behavior, encourage employee input, support risk-taking, recognize and appreciate employees' skills and efforts, and involve them in decision-making processes (Konopaske et al., 2018, p. 417). Introducing a Participating Leadership Style at MU holds significant potential to address the existing challenges by enhancing inclusion, aligning priorities, and improving employee motivation.

The implementation of a Participating Leadership Style at MU would yield desirable impact on MU's culture because it would allow MU leadership to:

i. Capitalize on faculty and staff readiness and potential

Strong participating leadership allows organizations to capitalize on the skills, ideas, and expertise of every member of the organization (Perriera, 2015). The senior leaders at MU could be trained to identify the strengths of the faculty and staff and recognize their level of readiness (i.e., their ability to be accountable for their self-directed behavior) so that roles and responsibilities can be assigned to them accordingly. Paying particular attention to issues of diversity and inclusion, for example, can encourage and support women who have shown readiness to take on leadership positions (Gustavo, 2018). Research shows that if women are given appropriate support in the form of direct mentorship and incentivized professional development opportunities, they can thrive in positions of power (Salazar, 2018; Sanders, 2017). Similarly, MU could benefit from creating leadership opportunities specifically for faculty and staff who demonstrate readiness and potential.

ii. Involve faculty staff and in decision-making

Leaders who involve employees in decision-making promote a more inclusive environment where employees feel a strong sense of belonging and job satisfaction (Hersey & Blanchard, 1988). In their empirical study of leadership decision-making in seven different successful companies, Jones and Acuto (2010) found a significant positive relationship between employee participation on committees and job satisfaction. For example, in one of the companies studied, employees who participated in at least one committee were three times as likely to report a high interest in extending their contract compared to those who did not participate in committees. Jones and Acuto (2010) also found that this involvement fostered openness in communication between superiors and employees. The leaders at MU could create committees composed of faculty and staff to discuss issues related to the university's operation and involve them in decision-making. This would allow the university to reestablish its priorities so that they become aligned with those that had contributed to its longstanding success.

iii. Increase faculty and staff motivation and engagement

When faculty and staff feel recognized for their strengths and experiences and are allowed to participate in decision-making, it is likely that they will be more motivated and engaged (Konopaske et al., 2018), which would lead to an improved climate overall. The adoption of a Participating leadership style has successfully increased faculty motivation in institutions that are similar to MU. For example, at the Great Western University this style resulted in productivity (e.g., increased faculty publications), decreased absenteeism, and an overall positive university climate (Ali & Smith, 2019). It is anticipated that the effect on MU faculty and staff would be similar.

Table 6.7: (Cont.)

Implementing a Participating Leadership Style will offer MU a more fitting and sustainable solution compared to the Transformational Leadership Style. This approach has the potential to positively impact inclusion, priorities, and employee motivation. By capitalizing on faculty and staff potential, involving them in decision-making, and increasing their motivation and engagement, MU can create a conducive environment for achieving its organizational goals and fostering a culture of inclusion, academic excellence, and collaboration.

4.3. Strategies That Can Be Used to Emphasize the Need to Persuade and Align the Reader Toward the Writer's Position

Drawing on Engagement (Martin & White, 2005), we also suggest emphasizing the need to persuade and align the reader toward the writer's position by making explicit the resources that can be used to do this. Such resources include the following:

- **modality** (e.g., *may, might, could*) to entertain other voices and perspectives by avoiding alienating the reader (e.g., *the company could implement X* vs. *the company must implement X*)
  Example: *Zappos could turn its potential problem into an opportunity by educating its employees on misbehavior. This approach could help Zappos increase its profits.*
- **citing authoritative outside voices** to support a course of action (e.g., *a study conducted by Wanberg & Mueller [2000] noted that . . .*)
- **counter** resources that narrow the range of acceptable positions to align the reader with the writer's stated position (e.g., *however, yet, but,* and *nevertheless*)
  Example: *Zappos could turn its potential problem into an opportunity by educating its employees on misbehavior. This approach could help Zappos increase its profits. However, the disadvantage of this approach would be . . .*
- **concede-counter** resources that acknowledge the possibility of an alternative perspective and bring the reader closer to the writer's perspective (e.g., *although, though, whereas, while*)
  Example: *Although offering a cultural program based on Kotter's model of change is time consuming, the employees' improved motivation and performance will be worth the time spent.*

To help students identify these resources, ask them to reread the sample recommendations section in Table 6.7. Ask questions such as the ones in Table 6.8.

Table 6.8: Sample Questions to Identify Resources That Can Be Used to Emphasize the Need to Persuade and Align the Reader Toward the Writer's Position

1. Does the writer use modality (e.g., *may, might, could*) to entertain other voices and perspectives by avoiding alienating the reader? If so, can you identify examples in the text?
2. Does the writer cite authoritative outside voices to support a course of action?
3. Does the writer use counter resources that align the reader to the writer (e.g., *however, yet, but,* and *nevertheless*)? If so, can you identify examples in the text?
4. Does the writer use concede-counter resources that acknowledge the possibility of an alternative perspective and bring the reader closer to the writer's perspective (e.g., *although, though, whereas, while*)? If so, can you identify examples in the text?

It is also important to help students use reasoning and justification resources (Hao, 2020; Martin, 1992) to effectively support a position. To do this, students can use logical relations of cause and effect (e.g., *because, as, thus,* and *therefore*), comparison (e.g., *On the other hand, the limitations of the first solution are less significant . . .*), and conditional reasoning (e.g., *If the company does this, it will . . .*).

To help students identify these resources, ask them to reread the sample recommendations section in Table 6.7. Ask questions such as the ones in Table 6.9.

Table 6.9: Sample Questions to Identify Reasoning and Justification Resources to Effectively Support a Position

1. Does the writer use logical relations of cause and effect (e.g., *because, as, thus,* and *therefore*) to effectively support their position? If so, can you identify examples in the text?
2. Does the writer use logical relations of comparison (e.g., *On the other hand, the limitations of the first solution are less significant . . .*) to effectively support their position? If so, can you identify examples in the text?
3. Does the writer use conditional reasoning resources to effectively support their position (e.g., *If the company does this, it will . . .*). If so, can you identify examples in the text? Are there any places in the text where the writer could have used these resources to support their position more effectively? Please re-write these parts and justify your choice of resources.

5. Concluding Remarks

In this chapter, we provided resources to help students write effective persuasive texts in classroom contexts where they are required to maintain a consistent stance while arguing for a preferred position among alternatives. Specifically, we showed how the Discussion genre from the Argument genre family can be used to achieve a persuasive purpose, and we presented strategies and linguistic resources that can be used to justify the benefits of a preferred option or alternative.

References

Coffin, C. (1996). *Exploring Literacy in School History*. Adult Migrant English Service.

Coffin, C. (2006). *Historical discourse: The language of time, cause and evaluation*. Continuum.

Hao, J. (2020). *Analyzing scientific discourse from a systemic functional perspective: A framework for exploring knowledge-building in biology*. Routledge.

Martin, J. R. (1992). *English text: System and structure*. John Benjamins.

Martin, J. R., & Rose, D. (2008). *Genre relations: Mapping culture*. Equinox.

Martin, J. R., & White, P. R. R. (2005). *The language of evaluation: Appraisal in English*. Palgrave Macmillan.

Nathan, P. (2016). Analysing options in pedagogical business case reports: Genre, process and language. *English for Specific Purposes*, *44*, 1–15.

Pessoa, S., Mitchell, T. D., & Gómez-Laich, M. P. (2023). Argument not optional: The language of alternatives and recommendations in the case analysis genre. *English for Specific Purposes*, *69*, 80–94.

CHAPTER 7

Tips for Assigning and Assessing Argumentative Writing

1. Overview

In this chapter, we discuss how to craft assignment guidelines and prompts that clearly align with the instructor's pedagogical expectations, and how to design assessment rubrics using the metalanguage presented in the book. Using sample assignment guidelines and prompts, we show how disciplinary teachers may not always be clear in their writing prompts and may not always set their students up for the targeted genre. We provide tips for instructors to ensure that their assignments are worded to elicit student uptake that aligns with their pedagogical goals.

We also show how genre and language expectations can be reflected in assessment rubrics. We share assessment rubrics informed by the 3x3 toolkit that highlight the importance of reviewing a text for its main argumentative purpose, organization, and argumentative linguistic resources at the whole text, paragraph, and phrase levels. Such careful review of student writing helps identify subtle ways in which students meet or do not meet genre expectations. We emphasize the importance of draft writing, feedback on drafts, individual consultations with students, joint construction with students using their drafts to show common problems and ways to address them, and redrafting based on feedback.

124

2. The Importance of Designing Assignment Guidelines and Prompts That Align With Pedagogical Expectations

Instructors need to make sure that they craft assignment guidelines and writing prompts that help students respond with the targeted genre. As we discussed in Chapter 2, sometimes instructors want students to engage in knowledge transformation (i.e., using disciplinary knowledge as a lens to identify and analyze problems in, for example, a case), but they use prompts that invite knowledge display (i.e., demonstrating understanding of a reading, a case, or disciplinary knowledge); and sometimes instructors have pedagogical goals that involve both knowledge display and knowledge transformation—a mix of description, analysis, and argument—but they craft assignment guidelines in ways that make it harder than necessary for students to meet expectations. Sometimes part of the solution can be small tweaks to the wording of the main question students are asked to respond to, and in some cases, assignment guidelines need to be revised more substantially.

In our research in disciplinary courses, we have worked with instructors to make the students' task as clear and explicit as possible. In this section, we present examples of *before* and *after* versions of writing prompts to illustrate revisions that our disciplinary collaborators have found useful to help their students respond to the assignment effectively. We also discuss how we have applied what we learned from these collaborations to our first-year writing classes.

3. The Importance of Word Choice in Prompts and Guidelines

In our research in history classrooms (Miller et al., 2016), we noticed that many students were responding to the writing prompts with non-argument genres when the professor wanted arguments. We analyzed the student responses to the six argumentative essays they wrote over a single semester and noticed a pattern. Most importantly, we noticed that small choices in the wording of prompts affected the likelihood that students

126   ANALYSIS AND ARGUMENT IN FIRST-YEAR WRITING AND BEYOND

would respond with an argument. Furthermore, we found that students were more likely to respond with an argument when asked to write about a primary source text. When asked to write about a historian's argument about historical information, they were more likely to summarize that author's argument rather than to create one of their own.

We found that the prompts most likely to elicit argument included direct address that asked for the student's perspective (*what sort of picture do you get...*) or were framed in terms of degree (*how compelling...*). When direct address is used, students are asked to go beyond re-presenting information from the source text by asserting their own position. When the prompt is framed in terms of degree, it invites the student to make an evaluative claim that then can be supported throughout the text. Table 7.1 shows some examples of prompts that use these strategies.

Table 7.1: Sample Prompts That Elicit Arguments

Argument
1. <u>How compelling</u> do <u>you</u> find the author's evidence that migration was slowed by ecological factors?
2. According to the author, <u>to what degree</u> does disease influence culture (i.e., religion)?
3. <u>What sort of picture do you get</u> about the treatment of Babylonian women based on <u>your</u> reading of the laws?

We found that prompts that were less likely to elicit argument were questions that asked about facts (*what happened when . . .*) or explanations (*what were the causes of . . .*). When the prompts are phrased in these ways, students are likely to interpret the assignment as an invitation to demonstrate their understanding of the reading rather than create an argument about it. Table 7.2 shows the original prompts and the revised versions that adopt the language more likely to elicit arguments.

Table 7.2: Original Prompts and Revised Versions That Adopt the Language More Likely to Elicit Arguments

Original	Revised
What happened when the four divergent disease pools began to mix at the start of the Christian era?	What <u>do you</u> think is the <u>most persuasive</u> evidence about the effects of the mixing of the disease pools at the start of the Christian era?

Tips for Assigning and Assessing Argumentative Writing

Table 7.2: (Cont.)

Original	Revised
Based on the narrative, what problems did Equiano face when he was enslaved by Africans?	To what extent do you think Equiano's treatment by African slave traders was better than his treatment by European ones?
What were the main causes of WWII?	How important was the role of Germany in causing WWII compared to the other countries that were involved?

Based on our research, when assigning writing based on source texts, we recommend the following:

1. Consider the sequence of assignments in the course, starting with source texts that more readily lend themselves to argumentative responses.
2. Model the process of responding effectively to a prompt about a secondary (argumentative) source with an argument (use examples that distinguish between summary and argument).
3. Be explicit about how the framing of questions of degree invites the students to make an evaluation and sustain an argument that remains focused on that evaluation; without this explicit instruction, students may simply elide the part of the question that asks about, for example, how compelling the evidence is and only provide a summary of the evidence.
4. Be explicit about the importance of responding to a prompt using the language provided in the original prompt (e.g., *To what extent to do you think Equiano's treatment by African slave traders was better than his treatment by European ones? Equiano's treatment by African slave traders was better than his treatment by European ones to a great extent*).

We can look at another example from a Case Analysis assignment in an introductory information systems course, where a slight change to the assignment was helpful. As you might recall from previous chapters, the Case Analysis is a written response that includes an analysis of an organization, using disciplinary concepts to identify problems or opportunities, followed by recommendations for enhancing the organization's practices. For this assignment, the instructor wanted the students to write a Case

128   ANALYSIS AND ARGUMENT IN FIRST-YEAR WRITING AND BEYOND

Analysis, but he kept referring to the assignment as an *essay* and only provided students with a set of questions to answer with little guidance about structure. Some of these questions asked for knowledge display—the instructor wanted students to demonstrate their understanding of the case. Other questions invited knowledge transformation—the instructor wanted the students to apply the disciplinary framework to the case. However, most students were demonstrating their understanding of the case without analyzing it. Table 7.3 shows the original question set with annotations for the type of response that is being solicited.

Table 7.3: Original Question Set and Type of Response Solicited

Original	Implied response types
Read the "Trouble in Legoland" article and answer the following questions: 1. In Poul's vision, what kind of innovation strategy was required for LEGO after 1998? 2. Was LEGO successful in their innovation attempts? What went wrong? How did they recover? 3. What does the phrase "binge of innovation [that occurred at LEGO]" imply? Read the Washington Post article and answer the following questions: 4. Briefly explain how LEGO has moved on to become the most innovative toy company in the world (in the opinion of the author). 5. Do you agree with the opinion of the author? Why or why not? (Support your answer by researching and finding two other articles or posts.)	1. Knowledge display: asks the student to show they understood what the author wrote 2. Knowledge transformation: asks the student to evaluate LEGO's success and analyze LEGO's use of innovation 3. Knowledge display: asks the student to define a term 4. Knowledge display: asks the student to summarize the author's opinion 5. Knowledge transformation: asks the student to take a position on the case and support it with authoritative voices

Table 7.4 shows an abbreviated version of the revised guidelines. The revisions include two significant changes: First, they provide a structure for students with the parts of a Case Analysis. Instead of just being structured as a set of questions, the revised assignment follows the structure of the Case Analysis genre. Second, the revisions separate the parts that require knowledge display from the parts that require knowledge transformation. By making these changes, the instructor was able to solicit a document that has the genre structure of a Case Analysis, rather than an essay or discrete answers to his questions, and the students were

Tips for Assigning and Assessing Argumentative Writing 129

able to understand more easily what was expected of them. The revised instructions emphasize in bold where the students are expected to report and describe, and where they are supposed to evaluate and analyze.

Table 7.4: Abbreviated Version of the Revised Guidelines

> <u>What is a case analysis?</u>
> A case analysis is a document in which you evaluate how a company dealt with a problem. In this case analysis, you will analyze the strategies that LEGO implemented to overcome its decline in sales and the extent to which they were successful or not. To do this, you will have to first explain the case in your own words. This means that you will have to **summarize** the problem(s) that LEGO faced and the solution(s) the company implemented. After this, you will have to **analyze** and **evaluate** the case. To do this, you are to rely on theoretical frameworks or key concepts learned in class. In this case, you will refer to the different approaches to innovation—e.g., incremental vs. radical innovation, process vs. product innovation, and stages of innovation (innovation diffusion). You will apply these concepts to analyze LEGO's innovation attempts and their degree of success/failure.
>
> **I. Introduction**
> In this section, you will introduce the case, analytical framework, and main argument from your analysis. Here are some guidelines . . .
>
> **II. Problems & Solutions (350–400 words)**
> In this section, you will select and **report** on the most important details of the LEGO company's history, as indicated in the three articles. You will need to briefly **describe** LEGO's major problems and their attempts at solving those problems. You may organize this section chronologically or by problem(s) and attempted solution(s).
>
> Consider the following questions when writing about the company's problems and attempted solutions.
>
> 1. What problems did LEGO encounter?
> 2. How did LEGO attempt to solve their problems?
> 3. What is the current state of the LEGO company?
>
> **IV. Analysis (550–600 words)**
> In this section, you will apply the disciplinary framework of innovation to **analyze** the strategies that LEGO implemented and **evaluate** the extent to which they were successful or not. In this section, you should:
>
> 1. Make a claim about the extent to which LEGO was successful or not in its approach to innovation. It's ok to have a nuanced analysis in which you indicate the degree to which LEGO was successful. In other words, you can say that it was somewhat successful or that it was successful in this area/aspect and not in another area/aspect.
> 2. Use the disciplinary framework of innovation to present and organize your ideas.
> 3. Define the relevant types of innovation for your analysis.
> 4. Provide evidence from the source text and outside sources to support your claim.
>
> **V. Conclusions & Recommendations (250 words)**
> 1. Sum up the main points from the case.
> 2. Discuss other possible innovation strategies that LEGO could have used.
> 3. State what other similar companies can learn from the experience of Lego.

130 ANALYSIS AND ARGUMENT IN FIRST-YEAR WRITING AND BEYOND

Based on our research, when the pedagogical goals entail a mix of knowledge display and knowledge transformation, we suggest that instructors call explicit attention to these different goals and provide students with a structured approach to meeting these goals.

4. The Importance of Avoiding Question Sets That Are Meant to Be Considered Holistically

We have found that when instructors provide a set of questions in their assignment guidelines, students often interpret them as an invitation to answer each question discretely. While such an interpretation might align with some instructors' expectations, we have observed that, in many cases, instructors provide the list to be considered holistically to help the student formulate a response that takes the questions into account in the planning phase of the writing process.

In one upper-level information systems course, the students were asked to write a particular Case Analysis assignment: the case development. This genre requires students to "develop" the case themselves. In other words, they write their own case rather than having the case provided to them. In this assignment, students were asked to visit a place that is a "designed experience" (e.g., a local museum; a library) and write a detailed narrative of their experience. This narrative then served as the data for the case as students analyzed it using relevant disciplinary frameworks. Students had to use a disciplinary framework to analyze their experience as they interacted with a museum's physical spaces and exhibits, then provide recommendations about how technology could be used to improve the overall user experience.

The instructor provided students with questions that were meant to help them take notes while they were at the museum, recording reflections about different aspects of their experience. Essentially, these questions were meant to scaffold the use of the disciplinary framework. In the written part of the analysis, the instructor expected the students to turn these reflections into an analysis of the overall user experience, but many students simply wrote discrete answers to the questions in paragraph form. As a result, their writing was not coherent and did not meet the expectations of abstracting their own experience to that of the average user.

The instructor felt it was important to preserve the question set, so in another iteration of the course we cowrote additional guidelines that made explicit how the questions were to be used during the museum visit

Tips for Assigning and Assessing Argumentative Writing 131

and when drafting the document students would submit. Table 7.5 shows an excerpt of the question set and the additional guidelines.

Table 7.5: Original Guiding Questions and Additional Guidelines

Excerpt of the guiding questions	Additional context for using the questions

Spatiotemporal
1. What effects do place and time have on our experience?
2. Did the technologies make you feel comfortable? Did you lose the sense of time?
3. Did you feel rushed?
4. What constraints were there related to the interactions with technologies?
 	
Compositional
1. How do the elements of an experience fit together to form a coherent whole? What technology elements were involved in each part?
2. Do you see a pattern to this?
	In your analysis, avoid the following:
	• organizing the text by time
	  Example: *When I arrived . . . when I entered)*
	• organizing the text by answers to the prompt questions in the order they were given
	  Example: *I did lose a sense of time when . . . . I felt rushed when . . .*
	
	In your analysis, do the following:
	• Evaluate the experience with depersonalized claims about how the environment shapes the user experience'
	  Example: *In McCarthy's framework, the compositional thread refers to . . . . Although there were many interesting objects at the museum (from old fancy cars to money from all over the world), the overall composition of the museum was not very coherent.*
	• Support these claims with the details of your experience.
	  Example: *Specifically, the overall floor plan and flow from room to room and the variety of objects found did not create a coherent experience . . .*

Before we provided the additional context in the guidelines, students would submit paragraphs that started with a sentence like: "*In the first half of the visit, I did feel rushed and completely lost the sense of time . . . . When I entered the last room, I felt rushed . . .*" In other words, they retold their narrative with answers to the questions; they evaluated their own experience instead of evaluating how the museum's design features shape the user experience and supporting these evaluations with details from their own experience.

Thus, based on this research, we suggest that instructors be explicit about their expectations for written work when they provide lists of questions to help with the prewriting process. Ideally, instructors should provide students with examples of discrete answers to a question set in conjunction with examples of the "final" written work so that students can see how the prewriting material can be effectively transformed into the target genre.

132   ANALYSIS AND ARGUMENT IN FIRST-YEAR WRITING AND BEYOND

We can consider another example from an upper-level organizational behavior assignment where, rather than being more explicit about how to use the question set, revisions were made to the wording of the prompt to ameliorate student challenges. As discussed in Chapter 6, students had to complete a Case Analysis assignment that asked them to discuss the advantages and disadvantages of two recommended solutions to solve an organization's problems, and to *argue* for the best recommendation. Students were challenged by the expectation to write effective recommendations while considering alternative solutions. Specifically, many students seemed to present the benefits and drawbacks of the two possible recommendations, then chose one without providing substantial argumentative reasoning for their choice.

We attribute this difficulty in meeting expectations, at least in part, to the phrasing and framing of the assignment guidelines (see Table 7.6 below). While the original questions do explicitly solicit an argument with reasoning for the best recommendation, the prompt seemingly could have done more to emphasize that argument is the primary purpose of the recommendations section; students' responses to these guidelines in their written work suggested that the three-question sequence did not do enough to foreground the argumentative expectations of the recommendations. We worked with the instructor to create a revised prompt that focuses on the need for an argument, then indicates how to support the argument with comparative reasoning. The revised assignment guidelines also provided supplementary information about specific strategies for comparative reasoning.

Table 7.6: Original and Revised Organizational Behavior Assignment

Original	Revised
1. What actionable options are available for resolving the key problem/opportunity? Provide two recommended options. 2. What are the advantages and disadvantages of each of the two recommended options? 3. What is the best recommendation? Why? Argue for this one recommended approach and explain why you recommend this approach for your case.	Argue for one recommended option by: • weighing the advantages and disadvantages of two viable options; • persuading the reader that the recommended option is the better of the two, and that its disadvantages are acceptable.

Based on this research, we suggest that instructors who provide a series of questions in their guidelines pay particular attention to the sequence and the hierarchy of importance of the questions. Instructors should foreground

Tips for Assigning and Assessing Argumentative Writing   133

the primary purpose of the assignment and be aware that students will likely structure their response according to the order of the questions.

5. The Importance of Having Consistent Parts in (First-Year Writing) Assignment Guidelines

When faculty assign multiple assignments in a course, we recommend that the assignment guidelines and writing prompts, if possible, follow a consistent format across the course, even when expectations for each assignment vary. This is important to help students become familiar with the expectations of the course as they are reminded of them throughout all the assignments.

For example, the three major assignments in one of our first-year writing classes start with an overview of the assignment that explains what students are expected to do. This is followed by:

- a rationale section that explains the skills the assignment helps students develop and the importance of those skills;
- a process section that gives students some tips on how to approach the assignment (e.g., *you may start by rereading the texts and reviewing your notes about how the arguments made by the authors we read connect to Bourdieu's capital*) and the stages in the process of completing the assignment (e.g., first draft, conference with instructor, second draft);
- an audience section that explains who will read the text and what they expect to find;
- a section that details the parts the assignment needs to have (an introduction, body paragraphs, and a conclusion); and
- a citations section that reminds students of the need to use APA style for their in-text citations and for the list of references.

Having a rationale section for each assignment in a writing class is particularly important because it helps students understand how the assignment fits into the assignment sequence in the course, what skill is being targeted and practiced, and how developing a given skill will help them with their writing beyond the course. This is important for students who may be skeptical about a particular writing course or an assignment.

Tables 7.7 and 7.8 show how we maintain this consistency across two of these assignments.

134 ANALYSIS AND ARGUMENT IN FIRST-YEAR WRITING AND BEYOND

Table 7.7: Analytical Synthesis Assignment Guidelines

Overview:
In this 3–4 double-spaced page analytical synthesis (approximately 1500 words), you will analyze inequality through the lens of Bourdieu's capital using the texts we have read and discussed this semester. While differences in economic capital clearly contribute to inequality through social class reproduction, many people may not be aware of the role of cultural and social capital in contributing to inequality. Thus, in your synthesis you will need to address the following question:

Beyond economic capital, how do cultural and social capital contribute to inequality? Rather than explain each author's individual argument, you will find common themes in the texts that help you explain how cultural and social capital contribute to inequality. You will group the authors accordingly, make claims about how their ideas about inequality relate to cultural and social capital, make connections, highlight similarities, and support your claims by synthesizing the authors' arguments.

Rationale:
The ability to synthesize information is important in academic writing; rarely is there one perspective, one voice, or one answer to an issue. Synthesis skills are necessary for producing a literature review. Literature reviews have different purposes. Often the purpose is to discuss the significance of the topic and broad areas of agreement or controversy (e.g., the status quo) to carve out a gap that an author will fill in that same text. But other times, the purpose is for an expert to synthesize scholarship on a big topic (like inequality) so others can see connections outside of their specialized field. And these often point to remaining questions or avenues of inquiry.

In your *analytical* synthesis, you will develop both your synthesizing and analytical skills. As we have seen with our discussion of the Onion Model in class, analyzing means breaking up something into its parts and seeing them through the lens of disciplinary knowledge. Throughout the first weeks of the semester, we have used the disciplinary knowledge/framework of Bourdieu's capital to tease out the various authors' arguments about inequality. Your job now is to use the concept of capital as the organizing principle of your analytical synthesis.

The ability to analyze using a disciplinary framework is an important skill to have. The analytical synthesis and the problem analysis assignments in this course will prepare you for the kinds of tasks you will be expected to do in many of your courses.

Process:
You may start by rereading the texts and reviewing your notes about how the arguments made by the authors we read connect to Bourdieu's capital. You should also review the discussion questions on Canvas and your own and your classmates' answers, the PowerPoint slides, and the Google docs we have used in our class discussions. You will then group the authors' ideas in terms of how they relate to cultural and social capital. Using the authors' ideas, you will make a claim about how cultural and social capital contribute to inequality. Throughout each paragraph, you will support your claims with evidence from the authors.

You will write a draft of your synthesis and receive feedback from your professor. You will use your professor's feedback to prepare your final draft.

Audience:
You should imagine that you are writing your analytical synthesis for an audience that is interested in inequality but that has NOT read the texts from our course. This means that you must make clear claims, precisely define and effectively use the terminology used by the authors, and provide relevant evidence from the authors to support your claims.

Tips for Assigning and Assessing Argumentative Writing 135

Table 7.7: (Cont.)

The Parts:

In your **introduction**, begin by introducing the significance of the topic of inequality using shared context with your audience. Shared context refers to something the audience knows and can relate to before you delve into inequality and capital. Be sure to convince your readers from the outset of the significance of the issue you are exploring—in other words, why should they care about inequality? Then preview your main argument and your supporting claims about how economic, cultural, and social capital and social class reproduction contribute to inequality.

Your claims in your **body paragraphs** will relate to how the different forms of capital contribute to inequality. But note that you don't necessarily have to have a separate paragraph to discuss social class reproduction. You may discuss social class reproduction in connection to the different forms of capital. . . .

Stay focused! Make sure that your paragraph is only about one topic and not multiple topics!

In your **conclusion**, you will need to reiterate the major points made in your synthesis and discuss wider implications by considering how, for example, the ideas presented may help you understand a specific case of inequality, or how you see inequality impacting your immediate context, or how you think inequality will play out in the future.

Citations:

Remember to integrate quotations and paraphrases from the authors we read—and only from these texts. However, quotations and paraphrases should not overwhelm your own analysis. Use APA style for your in-text citations and for your list of references. All the authors discussed in your paper need to be listed in your list of references.

Table 7.8: Problem Analysis Assignment Guidelines

Overview:

For your problem analysis, you will select a case related to inequality and you will analyze it through the lens of Bourdieu's capital and what we have learned about inequality this semester. A case could be the story of a person you know, a group of people, or a community; a current event; or a social phenomenon that points to a problem related to unequal access to economic, cultural, and/or social capital that contributes to social class reproduction and, ultimately, inequality. You will use your analysis of your case to argue about the complexities and characteristics of the problem(s) associated with the case or what the case represents. To support your position, you will draw on details of the case and the course readings.

Rationale:

As a student, you will be asked to apply disciplinary knowledge to analyze exemplars (e.g., cases) in many of your courses. As a future professional working as a consultant, you may be asked to study and analyze an organization or a problem faced by an organization to eventually provide solutions. Research shows that when posed with the challenging task of analyzing an exemplar, many students do not know how to approach the task and end up reporting disciplinary knowledge they learned in class or reporting on the case and do not necessarily engage in analysis. Thus, the problem analysis is aimed to help you develop analytical writing skills that will be of value to your future courses and careers.

(Continued)

136 ANALYSIS AND ARGUMENT IN FIRST-YEAR WRITING AND BEYOND

Table 7.8: (Cont.)

Process:

a. Selecting the case

The authors we have read this semester explore problems associated with inequality as they relate to specific cases. For example, Khan (2011) uses the case of St. Paul's to argue about issues of privilege among the elite in the United States. Lareau (2002, 2008, 2014) uses the case studies of middle-class and working-class families to analyze the impact of social class on child-rearing practices and the development of cultural and social capital. Rivera (2015) uses the case of hiring practices at prestigious consulting and law firms to argue about how elite students' cultural and social capital helps them to get elite jobs.

Here are some examples of potential cases:
• The college entrance examination in Chile
• Operation Varsity Blues: The College Admissions Scandal
• Privilege and inequalities in an education system or a school you are familiar with
• Privilege and inequalities based on citizenship
• Wasta in an institution or organization in the Arab world
• The inequalities associated with billionaires such as Jeff Bezos
• Inequalities associated with a socially marginalized group you are familiar with
Follow these guidelines when selecting a case.

Your case:
• needs to be limited in scope. For example, you may not write about all the problems in the educational system in your country. Instead, you can select one school and write about how this school represents broader issues of inequalities in your country.
• should be something that is presented as it is, as "raw data," without any analysis. For example, if it is a newspaper article, it should not be something that the author analyzes or makes arguments about. You are the one who needs to analyze the situation reported in the article using what you have learned about inequality.
• cannot be something that has been extensively reported on in the media: it probably cannot be something related to gender inequality or the challenges of African Americans during the pandemic because that's something that has been written about a lot in the last year.
• needs to be inspired by a key quote or a claim made by one of the authors we read this semester. This means that your case should be related to issues that we have read about this semester.
• may be based on your own personal experience if you can generate the data for the case by writing up a narrative of the experience or a description of the account based on your own personal experience or based on an interview with a relevant person. This will serve as the case that you will then analyze.
• should be used to represent wider social issues related to inequality. For example, the case of the college admissions scandal represents wider issues of privilege among the upper classes.

b. Analyzing your case:

The ability to analyze a case using a disciplinary framework and expert knowledge is an important skill to have. As we have seen with our discussion of the Onion Model, analyzing means breaking up something into its parts and seeing them through the lens of disciplinary knowledge.

Tips for Assigning and Assessing Argumentative Writing   137

Table 7.8: (Cont.)

This semester, we have used the disciplinary framework of Bourdieu's capital to tease out the various authors' arguments about inequality. Your job now is to use capital and our accumulated knowledge on inequality to tease apart your selected case and argue about the complexities and characteristics of your case and what your case represents as it relates to inequality. In your writing, you will use Bourdieu's capital and your knowledge about inequality to present and organize the information by making claims that use the key words from the expert knowledge you have gained this semester.

c. Researching your case and supporting your argument:
You will likely need to do some extra reading about your case to help you provide context and evidence in your argument. Collect information about your case from reliable sources of news such as reputable newspapers (e.g., *The New York Times*) and news channels such as Al Jazeera.

You will use the relevant course readings as a starting point for your analysis. In addition to using Bourdieu's text on capital, you will make connections to the course readings that most relate to your case. Depending on your topic, you are also responsible for finding one to three outside sources that specifically relate to the kinds of inequality your case represents. These sources will complement our course readings and will constitute your knowledge base for your analysis. Check Canvas for supplementary readings that may help you analyze your case, but also do your own research.

Organization:
Your argument will need to have three main parts developed into multiple paragraphs:
1. **An introduction that develops your case into an argument:** Following from the issue/problem/solution heuristic, you will focus on arguing for why your case poses a problem related to inequality. You need to provide contextual details about your case to show how it leads to a problem that relates to inequality. You may use stasis theory to frame your case as a problem of existence, definition, value, cause, and/or action. Your reader needs to be convinced that the problem is a real one and something must be done about it.
2. **An analysis section that draws on Bourdieu's capital and your knowledge about inequality to help you support your argument as you consider specific details about your case:** Use your topic sentences to make claims about your case using key words from Bourdieu's capital and the course readings on inequality. Support your claims by making specific connections between your case and the course readings and your own research. Use authors who would agree with your position about the case to strengthen your argument. To incorporate these authors effectively, you will need to be selective about what specific parts of their arguments you paraphrase or cite directly.
3. **A conclusion that helps your reader understand the larger implications of or potential solutions for your particular case:** Use the strategies for writing conclusions that we discussed this semester to help your reader understand why your argument is important beyond the particular case you analyzed.

Citations:
Use APA style for your in-text citations and for your list of references. All the authors discussed in your paper need to be listed in your list of references.

138 ANALYSIS AND ARGUMENT IN FIRST-YEAR WRITING AND BEYOND

6. Making Language Expectations Explicit in Assessment Rubrics

In this section, we show how genre and language expectations can be reflected in assessment rubrics. We share assessment rubrics informed by the 3x3 toolkit that highlight the importance of reviewing a text for its main argumentative purpose, organization, and argumentative linguistic resources at the whole text, paragraph, and phrase levels.

6.1. History Rubric

Based on our analysis of student writing and collaboration with faculty, we developed a strong understanding of the valued features of argumentative writing in history. After delivering writing workshops to make these features explicit to students, we saw the opportunity to build on the instructor's existing rubric with revisions that would link the workshop materials with the rubric's evaluative criteria. The rubric went through several iterations, each time becoming simpler, and thus more user-friendly, based on feedback from the instructor and students.

Based on Dreyfus et al. (2016), the rubric in Table 7.9 focuses the grader first on evaluating the essay as a whole text (purpose), then on the stages of argument (structure), then on the development of the supporting paragraphs (argumentative support), and finally on the conventions of academic writing (presentation). The rubric makes explicit that an argumentative thesis asserts a characterization or evaluation of history with supporting claims that are previewed in the introduction. The rubric highlights the use of linguistic resources to create logical flow (e.g., repetition of key words) and show logical connections (e.g., conjunctions for establishing cause and effect). The rubric also highlights the use of Engagement (Martin & White, 2005) resources to develop an argumentative stance. While it captures less information than our 3x3 description of history arguments presented in Chapter 1 (e.g., the descriptions of word-level language resources are less extensive; less emphasis is placed on language for creating logical connections), the rubric is designed to provide a level of detail that is manageable for both students and graders and to focus on the features of history arguments that are most important for students to control.

Tips for Assigning and Assessing Argumentative Writing 139

Table 7.9: History Rubric

Purpose Analytical argumentative response	1. The text provides a relevant answer to the prompt framed as an argumentative thesis with supporting claims. 2. The argumentative thesis asserts a characterization or evaluation of historical phenomena based on accurate interpretation of source text(s). 3. The argument is based on original analysis of the source text(s) and historical period and goes beyond reproducing information from the source text(s) by reorganizing the information to support the argument. 4. The text incorporates evaluations consistently to develop the same position from beginning to end.	Meets expectations	Developing expectations	Below expectations
Structure Clear stages and use of key words to keep the reader on track	1. The introduction previews the supporting claims, and these claims appear in the same order in the body. 2. The supporting claims are labeled using abstract nouns and discipline-specific vocabulary using the same/similar key words from the introduction. 3. The body paragraphs begin by stating a supporting claim and articulating how it supports the thesis. 4. The conclusion provides a consistent reinforcement of the thesis and main support by repeating key language from the text.	Meets expectations	Developing expectations	Below expectations

(Continued)

140   ANALYSIS AND ARGUMENT IN FIRST-YEAR WRITING AND BEYOND

Table 7.9: (Cont.)

| Development Argumentative support | 1. Paragraphs move from an abstract claim to concrete evidence to an abstract summation of the claim and use connectors to create a logical flow of information (e.g., repetition of key words, this/that, old before new, transitions).
2. Each paragraph focuses on a single supporting claim and uses words such as *because, since, so, thus, as a result of* to show the logical connections between ideas.
3. Paragraphs effectively integrate relevant and sufficient information or quotes from the source text(s) using "opening" phrases (*According to X, X argues that*) and show how the information supports the thesis and supporting claims using "narrowing" phrases (*this shows, this means*).
4. Paragraphs consistently support the argument while showing awareness of and/or refuting alternative perspectives using language such as *although this/that, may, can, seem, possibly.* | Meets expectations | Developing expectations | Below expectations |
| Presentation Attention to academic conventions | 1. The register (tone) is appropriate to the assignment (avoids conversational style).
2. The text uses standard grammar, spelling, and punctuation.
3. The text uses clear and concise language with appropriate word choice.
4. The text uses consistent citations. | Meets expectations | Developing expectations | Below expectations |

Tips for Assigning and Assessing Argumentative Writing 141

6.2. Information Systems Rubric

Table 7.10 shows the rubric for the LEGO Case Analysis assignment discussed in Section 7.2.1. We took a similar approach as with the history rubric but tailored it to the Case Analysis genre and the requirements of the assignment. In this rubric, under Purpose and Structure, each criterion corresponds to one of the major sections of the assignment (Introduction, Background, Analysis, Recommendations). The criteria under Development are focused on the valued features found through our analysis of student texts; specifically, these are ideational resources (logical relations, relevant evidence, source use) and interpersonal resources (consistent evaluations, awareness of alternative perspectives).

Table 7.10: Information Systems Rubric

Purpose Analyzes and evaluates the case	1. The text makes a sound overall evaluation of the case using relevant concepts from the disciplinary framework. 2. The text clearly and accurately represents LEGO's problems and implemented solutions. 3. The text supports the evaluation consistently with relevant and accurate evidence from the case and outside sources. 4. The text provides solutions/recommendations consistent with the analysis and evaluation that could be actionable by a company other than LEGO.	Meets expectations	Developing expectations	Below expectations
Structure Includes all major sections and uses key words to keep the reader on track	1. The introduction provides concise background information (about the case and the analysis) and establishes a structure for the document.	Meets expectations	Developing expectations	Below expectations

(Continued)

142 ANALYSIS AND ARGUMENT IN FIRST-YEAR WRITING AND BEYOND

Table 7.10: (Cont.)

	2. The problem/solution section is organized chronologically OR by problems and attempted solutions. 3. The analysis section's paragraphs have topic sentences that point back to the introduction's language and overall evaluation AND focus on an element of the disciplinary framework. 4. The recommendations are based on the analysis and use the same/similar words that are presented in the analysis.			
Development Analytical argumenta- tive support	1. The major body paragraphs use the know-see-conclude heuristic to show how the analysis is anchored in disciplinary knowledge and supported by case evidence. 2. Analysis paragraphs focus on a credible claim and maintain consistent evaluations to support it throughout. 3. Analysis paragraphs effectively integrate relevant evidence from the case and support from credible sources that show how the information supports the overall evaluation. 4. Analysis paragraphs consistently position the reader while showing awareness of and/or refuting alternative perspectives.	Meets expectations	Developing expectations	Below expectations

Tips for Assigning and Assessing Argumentative Writing

Table 7.10: (Cont.)

| Presentation Attention to academic conventions | 1. The writer includes appropriate subheadings for each section. 2. The writer presents ideas clearly and concisely. 3. The writer uses standard grammar with attention to word choice, sentence structure, subject-verb agreement, punctuation, and spelling. 4. The writer cites references appropriately and consistently. | Meets expectations | Developing expectations | Below expectations |

6.3. First-Year Writing Rubric

Table 7.11 shows a rubric that we designed for the purpose of our first-year writing course to assess an Analytical Synthesis assignment and a Problem Analysis assignment. In the Synthesis assignment, the students have to use the disciplinary framework of Bourdieu's capital to analyze inequality using the texts that we read and discuss in the course, connecting the authors using Bourdieu's framework. In the Problem Analysis assignment, the students are asked to choose a case and analyze it through the lens of Bourdieu's capital and the course readings on inequality, arguing how the case represents a problem related to inequality. These major expectations are reflected in the Purpose section of the rubric. The Structure section is mostly concerned with the overall structure of the text, including the major parts of an argument with paragraphs that move from abstract claims anchored in disciplinary knowledge to concrete information from the course readings in the Synthesis and from the case in the Problem Analysis. The Development criterion highlights the importance of writing consistent analytical paragraphs that start with abstract topic sentences anchored in disciplinary knowledge and supported with concrete information (from the sources or the case), effectively integrating multiple voices and demonstrating an awareness of multiple perspectives and aligning the reader with the writer's position.

144 ANALYSIS AND ARGUMENT IN FIRST-YEAR WRITING AND BEYOND

Table 7.11: Problem Analysis Rubric

Purpose Analytical argumentative response	1. The paper has a significant central argument that clearly addresses an identified problem within a broader issue and shows that the writer's sophisticated analysis is anchored in relevant disciplinary knowledge. 2. The ideas in the paper are coherent, relevant, and consistently support the central argument. 3. There is both convincing and sufficient evidence to support the author's claims and to develop the argument.	Meets expectations	Developing expectations	Below expectations
Structure Clear stages and use of key words to keep the reader on track	1. The paper has clear sections and goes beyond listing points to create connections between ideas. 2. There is a sense of logical flow for the reader. The central argument is introduced using shared context and claims are previewed in the introduction using relevant disciplinary concepts. 3. The paper demonstrates that the author has an accurate and sophisticated understanding of how disciplinary concepts should be used to present and organize information.	Meets expectations	Developing expectations	Below expectations
Development Argumentative support	1. Each body paragraph focuses on one topic, and paragraphs are developed so that sentences flow from abstract to concrete.	Meets expectations	Developing expectations	Below expectations

Tips for Assigning and Assessing Argumentative Writing

Table 7.11: (Cont.)

	2. Topics sentences are anchored in disciplinary concepts, and paragraphs maintain the author's consistent evaluations throughout. 3. The paragraphs effectively integrate multiple voices to show how the author supports their analysis using disciplinary knowledge and evidence, demonstrating an awareness of multiple perspectives and aligning the reader with the writer's position.			
Presentation Attention to academic conventions	1. The paper presents ideas clearly, precisely, and concisely using standard conventions for academic communication, including grammatically complete sentences and attention to word choice. 2. The paper cites references appropriately and consistently.	Meets expectations	Developing expectations	Below expectations

Final Grade:

A	shows sophisticated control in all the areas targeted by the above criteria and impresses the grader by letting them think about the argument and insights into disciplinary knowledge rather than focus on how the paper is written
A-	is strong in criteria related to purpose and analysis but may show occasional minor problems with structure/organization and paragraph development; writer may appear to be a risk-taker who sometimes makes mistakes when trying to express a difficult concept or play with language

(*Continued*)

146 ANALYSIS AND ARGUMENT IN FIRST-YEAR WRITING AND BEYOND

B+	has a clear and organized but not impressively complex, significant, or well-supported argument and analysis; demonstrates good understanding of disciplinary knowledge; controls presentation conventions generally well with only occasional lapses
B	makes a clear and organized but not necessarily significant or well-supported argument; demonstrates adequate understanding of disciplinary knowledge; presentation does not distract grader
B-	makes a clear and organized argument but may only partially support it or convince the grader of its validity; may sometimes misinterpret disciplinary knowledge or fail to see relations between disciplinary ideas; may exhibit more frequent lapses in presentation conventions
C+	makes an argument but then may stray from it; demonstrates only a partial or very superficial understanding of disciplinary knowledge; may have more frequent instances where language or presentation conventions distract the grader
C	fails to create a unifying argument; may appear to be more of a list with each paragraph having a separate argument; may suffer from lapses of language or failure to follow conventions that make portions of the text difficult to understand
Note: Any grade below a C indicates an immediate need to seek help from the Academic Resource Center before submitting the next paper.	
C-	contains claims related to the topic that are not always supported and that do not come together into a coherent argument; language and presentation issues (verb agreement, use of articles, word choice, spelling, capitalization, and punctuation) seriously distract the grader from the writer's intended message
D+	may demonstrate a failure to take the assignment seriously as evidenced by a failure to develop ideas or follow the instructions in the assignment; may have large sections of the paper that language issues render difficult to interpret; may show potential for what the writer could have done
D	represents a serious lack of effort on the part of the student and only a basic attempt to meet the requirements of the assignment
F	completely unsatisfactory effort on the part of the student or complete lack of awareness for how to construct a coherent piece of writing

7. Applying the Teaching Learning Cycle: Drafting, Feedback, and Negotiated Construction

The Teaching Learning Cycle (TLC) (Rothery, 1996) is an interactive and iterative writing-focused pedagogical cycle of teaching and learning activities framed within Systemic Functional Linguistics (SFL) genre pedagogy that includes three main stages: deconstruction, joint construction, and independent construction of text. In the deconstruction phase, the teacher engages students in analyzing a mentor text's purpose, stages, and language. In joint construction, students practice writing the target genre with their teacher in preparation for independent construction. During independent construction, teachers can meet with students individually in person or online and continue to offer support and feedback (de Oliveira & Smith, 2019).

As the activities provided in each chapter of this book indicate, our approach to scaffolding student writing emphasizes deconstruction: the analysis of effective and less effective sample texts with students in class. When it is time for students to write on their own (the independent construction stage), we include further support through cycles of drafting, feedback, and negotiated construction. In higher education (where there is little time to engage in joint construction of texts), negotiated construction after the teacher has provided feedback on students' first drafts may be more feasible and beneficial than joint construction. Our research shows that the inclusion of cycles of feedback and negotiated construction within independent construction is particularly important because the deconstruction of texts may not be enough for students to meet genre expectations; in negotiated construction, the students work with their own texts, which is likely to generate more investment from the students (see Gómez-Laich et al., 2023).

Offering one-on-one consultations may not be feasible for many instructors because of time constraints, as they involve personalized interaction and feedback tailored to each student's needs. If individual consultations are not feasible, alternative approaches such as group sessions may be more practical for instructors to engage with a larger number of students effectively.

8. Concluding Remarks

In this chapter, we have provided suggestions on how to craft assignment guidelines and prompts that clearly align with the instructor's pedagogical expectations and how to design assessment rubrics using the metalanguage presented in the book. We hope that the materials we have provided in this book—analytical tools, accessible metalanguage for unpacking features of student writing, sample exercises, and rubrics—can be of use to instructors. We encourage readers to adapt these materials to their own contexts. We also encourage readers to delve into the SFL scholarship that grounds our work; while it can seem intimidating to newcomers, SFL theory can be approached a little bit at a time, suiting particular needs as they arise. The impact of explicit SFL instruction is extremely beneficial to students, so we hope that teachers make use of the tools presented in this book to help their students write effective arguments.

References

de Oliveira, L. C., & Smith, S. (2019). Interactions with and around texts: Writing in elementary schools. In N. Caplan & A. Johns (Eds.), *Changing practices for the L2 writing classroom: Moving beyond the five-paragraph essay* (pp. 65–88). University of Michigan Press.

Dreyfus, S., Humphrey, S., Mahboob, A., & Martin, J. M. (2016). *Genre pedagogy in higher education. The SLATE project.* Palgrave Macmillan.

Gómez-Laich, M. P., Pessoa, S., & Mahboob, A. (2023). Writing development of the case analysis genre: The importance of feedback and negotiated construction in the Teaching Learning Cycle. In D. Zhang, & R. T. Miller (Eds.), *Crossing boundaries in researching, understanding, and improving language education: Essays in honor of G. Richard Tucker* (pp. 169–188). Springer.

Martin, J. R., & White, P. R. R. (2005). *The language of evaluation.* Palgrave Macmillan.

Miller, R. T., Mitchell, T. D., & Pessoa, S. (2016). Impact of source texts and prompts on students' genre uptake. *Journal of Second Language Writing, 31,* 11–24.

Rothery, J. (1996). Making changes: Developing an educational linguistics. In R. Hasan & G. Williams (Eds.), *Literacy in society* (pp. 86–123). Longman.

Index

abstractions, 52–53, 60

acknowledge moves, 93, 97, 119

analysis (discourse pattern), 26–28. *related lessons,* 28–46; identifying when an assignment calls for description, analysis, or argument, 40–41; moving from knowledge display to knowledge transformation, 28–39; understanding analysis and argument using visualization, 41–46

analysis, process of: applying disciplinary frameworks in, 13–17, 26–28, 41–43, 46; ideational meanings and resources in, 14–17, 19, 14; making evaluations in, 49, 51, 55; using 3x3 to unpack, 13–17; visualizing, 41–46. *related lessons:* analyzing cases, generating key words, and writing claims, 63–64

Analytical Synthesis: sample assessment rubric for, 143–46; sample assignment guidelines for, 134–35. *related lessons:* identifying Engagement resources, 100–102

analytical writing: assessing, 138–46; assigning (*see* assignment guidelines); challenges in, 67–71; connecting knowledge and data in (*see* know-see-conclude heuristic); disciplinary frameworks in, 14; engaging readers in, 91–96; ideational meanings and resources in, 14–17, 19, 141; knowledge transformation *vs.* display in, 29–30, 32–33; waves of meaning in, 76–79; writing claims in (*see* claims, writing). *related lessons,* 73–85; identify *know, see,* and *conclude* moves, 81–85; practice with identifying flatlines of meaning, 80–81; visualizing effective waves of meaning, 76–79; visualizing information flow to avoid flatlines of meaning, 73–76. *See also* Case Analysis; Problem Analysis

argument (discourse pattern), 26, 28. *related lessons,* 28–46; identifying when an assignment calls for description, analysis, or

argument, 40–41; moving from knowledge display to knowledge transformation, 28–39; understanding analysis and argument using visualization, 41–46;
argument (term usage), 3
argumentative writing: analysis process and (*see* analysis, process of); assessing, 138–46; assigning (*see* assignment guidelines); conceptualizing, 1–8; diagnosing challenges in, 11–13; engaging readers in, 91–96; ideational resources and meanings in, 13, 14, 141; interpersonal meanings and, 9–13; knowledge transformation in (*see* knowledge transformation *vs.* knowledge display); multiple perspectives in (*see* writer's perspective, aligning readers with); reader expectations in, 48, 51, 86, 91, 95, 97; scaffolding, 1, 14–20, 147; writing claims in (*see* claims, writing). *See also* Case Analysis
Argument genre, 1–8, 28. *See also* Case Analysis
assessment rubrics, 138–46
assignment guidelines: consistent parts in, 133–37; question sets in, 130–33; word choice in, 125–30; writing claims using language of, 54–55
assignment prompts: analyzing and understanding, 40–41;

designing, 125–33; multiple perspectives invited by, 104–7; writing claims using language of, 54–55
Attribute-Endorse, 94, 95–96, 100
attribute moves, 94, 95–96, 100. *See also* Attribute-Endorse
authoritative voices: integrating to support arguments, 68, 86, 88–89; justifying a preferred position with, 111, 121

Background (Case Analysis), 17
bare assertions, 93, 100

Case Analysis: assessment rubric for, 141–43; connecting disciplinary knowledge with data in, 70–71; defined, 14, 25–26; disciplinary frameworks in, 14–17, 19, 28; knowledge transformation in, 26, 29–31; stages of, 17; 3x3 scaffolding of, 17–19; visualizing analysis process for, 41–43
causal relations, 51, 55, 57
Challenge (argument genre type), 2
claims, defined, 51–52; claims, writing, 48–65; challenges in, 49–51; making evaluations in, 49, 51, 55, 57–58; using causal relations in, 51, 55, 57; using disciplinary key words in, 51, 52–58; using language from prompts in, 54–55; using main and supporting claims in, 48, 59–61. *related lessons,* 61–65; analyzing cases, generating

Index

151

key words, and writing
claims, 63–64; identifying
components of effective
claims, 62–63; revising claims,
64–65; which claim is more
effective?, 61–62
Concede-Counter, 94, 96, 99, 100,
111, 121
conclude moves, 77–79, 81–85
counter-expectational words,
91, 95, 97
counter moves: Concede-Counter,
94, 96, 99, 100, 111, 121;
counter-expectational words,
91, 95, 97; in Engagement
framework, 94; in justifying a
preferred position, 104, 111,
121; omission of, 108–9
critique (discourse pattern), 26, 28

deconstruction stage (TLC),
20, 147
definitions, disciplinary, 51
deny moves, 94
description (discourse pattern),
26–28. *related lessons,*
28–46; identifying when
an assignment calls for
description, analysis, or
argument, 40–41; moving
from knowledge display to
knowledge transformation,
28–39; understanding
analysis and argument using
visualization, 41–46
dialogic expansion and narrowing,
92, 93–94, 95–96
disciplinary frameworks:
in analysis process,

13–17, 26–28, 41–43, 46;
in analytical writing, 7;
in argumentative writing,
28; challenges applying,
16–17; defined, 13–14, 26;
disciplinary key words and,
53–54, 56; examples of,
27–28; ideational meanings
and, 14; in knowledge
transformation, 26–28.
related lessons: discussing
sample texts, 38; moving
from knowledge display to
knowledge transformation,
28–39; other activities, 41
disciplinary knowledge, connecting
data with, 28, 67, 68–71
discourse patterns, 26, 28
Discussion genre, 2, 109–12.
related lessons: deconstructing
sample texts, 111–18;
drafting, 20, 147

emergent arguments, 11–13
endorse moves, 93, 94, 95–96,
97, 100
engagement. *See* writer's
perspective, aligning
readers with
Engagement framework:
aligning readers with
writer's perspective using,
91–96; justifying a preferred
position using, 111, 121–22.
related lessons: identifying
Engagement resources,
98–102; revising texts
using Engagement
resources, 102

engagement moves, 93–94

evaluations: in justifying a preferred position, 104, 105, 111, 112, 114; supporting, 28; in writing claims, 49, 51, 55, 57–58

expanding the dialog, 92, 93, 94, 95–96

Exposition, 2. *See also* argumentative writing; Argument genre

feedback, 20, 147

flatlines of meaning: avoiding, 73–76; identifying, 80–81; *vs.* waves of meaning, 76–79

genre expectations: communicating, 2, 6, 20–21 (*see also* assessment rubrics); interpersonal, ideational, and textual resources in, 11–13; students' difficulty meeting, 3–6, 11–13. *See also* specific genres

genres, academic, 2, 4–11, 13, 91

grammatical metaphors, 52–53

ideational meanings and resources: in academic genres, 5, 6–7, 9, 13; in analytical writing, 14–17, 19, 141; in argumentative writing, 13, 14, 141; assessing use of, 141; defined, 4

ideational metafunction, 1

independent construction stage (TLC), 20–21, 147

information flow, 5, 73–79, 83, 138

interpersonal meanings and resources: in academic genres, 5, 7–8, 9–11, 141; in argument, 9–13, 14, 34; assessing use of, 141; defined, 4; handling multiple perspectives with, 10, 86. *See also* evaluations

interpersonal metafunction, 1–2

Issue stage (Discussion genre), 110, 111–12. *related lessons:* deconstructing sample texts, 111–18

joint construction stage (TLC), 20, 21, 147

justification of one position among alternatives, 104–23; challenges in, 104–9, 110–11; Discussion genre writing in, 2, 109–121 strategies for, 118; using Engagement framework in, 111, 121–22; using logical relations in, 122. *related lessons,* 111–23; deconstructing sample texts, 111–18; strategies for emphasizing need for persuasion and alignment, 121–22; strategies for justifying the benefits of a preferred option or alternative, 118–21

justification resources, 122

key words, disciplinary: abstractions as, 52–53; connecting, 51, 52, 55;

Index

generating, 46, 53–55, 56–58, 63–64; grammatical metaphors as, 52–53; packaging information with, 51, 52; writing claims using, 51, 52–58, 63–64. *related lessons:* analyzing cases, generating key words, and writing claims, 63–64

knowledge, connecting to data, 28, 67, 68–71

knowledge display, 12, 24

knowledge transformation *vs.* knowledge display, 24–47; academic expectations and, 27–28; applying disciplinary frameworks for, 26–28; challenges in, 12, 24, 25–26; using Onion Model for, 24, 26, 28, 41–43. *related lessons,* 28–46; identifying when an assignment calls for description, analysis, or argument, 40–41; moving from knowledge display to knowledge transformation, 28–39; other activities, 41; understanding analysis and argument using visualization, 41–46

know moves, 81–85

know-see-conclude heuristic: logical relations in, 71–73; visualization of, 72, 73–79, 83. *related lessons,* 73–85; identifying flatlines of meaning, 80–81; identifying *know, see,* and

conclude moves, 81–85; visualizing effective waves of meaning, 76–79; visualizing information flow to avoid flatlines of meaning, 73–76

language, SFL conceptualization of, 1–2

linking relations, 51

logical relationships, 71–73, 122, 138. *related lessons:* know-see-conclude heuristic, 73–85

meaning(s): flatlines of, 74; ideational (*see* ideational meanings and resources); interpersonal (*see* interpersonal meanings and resources); SFL conceptualization of, 1–2, 4–5; textual, 4, 5, 6, 8, 9; waves of, 76–79. *related lessons,* 73–81; visualizing effective waves of meaning, 76–79; visualizing information flows to avoid flatlines of meaning, 73–76, 80–81

modality, 93, 95, 97, 111, 121

multi-voiced statements, 92–94. *related lessons:* distinguishing from single-voiced texts, 96–98

narrowing the dialog, 92, 93–94, 95–96

negotiated construction, 20–21, 147

154 INDEX

Onion Model: analysis process and, 41–43; knowledge transformation and, 24, 26, 28; writing claims using, 51. *related lessons,* 28–46; discussing sample texts, 31, 38; identifying when an assignment calls for description, analysis, or argument, 40–41; moving from knowledge display to knowledge transformation, 28–39; other activities, 41; showing discourse patterns in sample texts, 35–39; visualizing analysis process before writing, 41–46

paragraphs, logical movement in, 49–51

PEEL (Point, Elaboration, Evidence, Link), 49

perspectives, multiple: challenges of managing, 86, 104–9; using Engagement framework for, 95, 111; writing effective Discussion genre for, 2, 109–10. *See also* writer's perspective, aligning readers with

Perspective stages (Discussion genre), 110, 112. *related lessons:* deconstructing sample texts, 111–18

Problem Analysis: identifying discourse patterns in, 36–39; sample assessment rubric for, 143–46; sample assignment guidelines for, 135–37; using 3x3 toolkit to scaffold, 17–19; visualizing analysis process for, 43–46; writing claims for, 57–58

problem-solution paper, 105

prompts. *See* assignment prompts

pronounce moves, 93, 95

question sets, 130–33

readers' perspectives and expectations: argumentative writing and, 48, 51, 86, 91, 95, 97; engaging (*see* writer's perspective, aligning readers with)

reader–writer relationship, 95–96

reasoning resources, 122

Reinforcement (Case Analysis), 17

Resolution stages (Discussion genre), 110, 112. *related lessons:* deconstructing sample texts to show how to meet genre expectations, 111–18

Revision. *related lessons:* revising claims, 64–65; revising texts using Engagement resources, 102

rubrics. *See* assessment rubrics

single-voiced statements, 92–94. *related lessons:* distinguishing between single- and multi-voiced texts, 96–98

Index

Systemic Functional Linguistics (SFL), xv–xvi, 1–2, 109. *See also* Teaching Learning Cycle; 3x3 toolkit

Teaching and Learning Cycle (TLC), 20–21, 147
textual meanings and resources, 4, 5, 6, 8, 9. *See also* information flow; paragraphs, logical movement in
textual metafunction, 2
thesis: as Argument genre feature, 2–3; in assessment rubrics, 138; as Case Analysis genre stage, 17; disciplinary frameworks and, 19; supporting claims for, 48, 59–61. *See also* claims, writing
3x3 toolkit: adapting to academic genres, 4–11; analysis process breakdown using, 13–17; assessment rubrics informed by, 138; behind-the-scenes use of, 20; conceptualizing argumentative writing with, 1, 3–8; diagnosing challenges with argument using, 11–13; interpersonal meanings and, 9–13; scaffolding

argumentative writing using, 17–19, 20
transcategorization, 52–53

voice, single- *vs.* multi-, 92–94. *related lessons:* distinguishing between single- and multi-voiced texts, 96–98
voices, authoritative, 68, 86, 88–89, 111, 121

waves of meaning, 76–79
writer's perspective, aligning readers with, 86–103; challenges in, 86–91; interpersonal resources for, 10, 86; using Engagement framework for, 91–96; using small language choices for, 92, 95–96. *related lessons:* distinguishing between single- and multi-voiced texts, 96–98; identifying Engagement resources, 98–102; revising texts using Engagement resources, 102; strategies for emphasizing need for persuasion and alignment, 121–22
writing prompts. *See* assignment prompts